THE CONTENTS OF THE BASKET

The Contents of the Basket

And Other Papers on
Children's Books and Reading

Edited by

FRANCES LANDER SPAIN

New York

The New York Public Library

1960

The lectures collected in this volume were given at The New York Public Library on the following dates:

Taro Yashima	15 November 1954
Annis Duff	22 May 1956
William Pène du Bois	19 November 1956
Elizabeth Gray Vining	24 April 1957
Elizabeth Enright	18 November 1957
Ruth Sawyer	14 April 1958
Amelia Munson	14 April 1959
Harry Behn	9 November 1959
Elizabeth Nesbitt	28 April 1960

The papers of Taro Yashima and Harry Behn are reprinted by permission from *The Horn Book Magazine,* in which they appeared in February 1955 and in April 1960, respectively.

Reprinted from the *Bulletin of The New York Public Library* are the papers of William Pène du Bois (April 1957), Elizabeth Gray Vining (September 1957), Annis Duff (October 1957), and Elizabeth Enright (May 1958).

Woodcuts by Palmer Brown.

Library of Congress Catalog Card Number: 60–53296

Preface

A SERIES *of spring lectures on children's books and children's reading was inaugurated in 1956 in the Donnell Library Center Auditorium. That first lecture was one of the events marking the fiftieth anniversary of the establishment, in 1906, of a Department of Library Work with Children by The New York Public Library and of the appointment of Anne Carroll Moore as its first superintendent. The lecture series was planned as an annual program for adults generally or professionally interested in books and library work for children. It was expected that these lectures would be gathered together at irregular intervals and offered in printed form.*

Five spring lectures have now been given, each presenting a different and important aspect of the general topic. The series began with Annis Duff's delightful account of a family enjoying books and reading together. It went across the ocean with Elizabeth Gray Vining's vivid description of the reading experiences and opportunities of Japanese children as she had observed them. The next year Ruth Sawyer discussed books as sources from which the storyteller draws his magic. Miss Sawyer proved that books are to be heard as well as read, in the storytelling with which she closed her lecture. Then, to that oft-asked question "Do children really like poetry now?", Amelia Munson answered an emphatic "Yes!" Quoting lines and whole poems, she demonstrated her method of presenting poetry to groups of children. In the most recent lecture, Elizabeth Nesbitt summed up the philosophy of book selection which underlies all good book service to children.

In addition to these lectures, four papers have been included for the further illumination they bring to the subject. These are papers that have been presented at the annual opening of the Exhibition of Children's Books Suggested as Holiday Gifts, held each November in the Central Children's Room of the Fifth Avenue Building of the Library. In her paper Elizabeth Enright traced the changing attitudes of society as reflected in the characters in children's books.

Harry Behn and Taro Yashima recounted the influences that contributed to their development as author-artists, and William Pène du Bois recreated the creation of his LION in hilarious fashion.

The Library expects to continue the two annual programs at which these lectures were given and looks forward to the future publication of a second volume of papers when another basket of them has accumulated.

December 5, 1960

Contents

Introduction

CHILDREN'S librarians would pick up the theme of Mrs Vining's folk-tale and would fill the basket with an inexhaustable supply of children's books so that there would be no question of what it contained. There would be books that set a child's imagination afire, that free his spirit, that enrich his mind, those to reveal the child to himself, others to give him understanding of his neighbor, and some to delight him with pure pleasure. In the basket would be books that have style in writing, distinction in illustration and design, quality in contents, books that speak to the child with respect and that leave him with satisfactions from his reading.

To keep the basket full of the right books, the children's librarians should be ever alert to identify the outstanding, distinguished ones, firm in their determination to reject those that are shoddy and mediocre, and tireless in their efforts to introduce childen and books. In this day of slipshod performances and a general deterioration of society, it is imperative that children find books that, themselves, represent honesty and integrity and that reflect in their contents, whether fiction or information, the high standards which have been developed.

For fifty years or more, children's books have been written, illustrated, edited, and published in a climate that recognized quality, that emphasized the individuality of the book and of the potential reader, that encouraged each author to create to the utmost of his skill and abilities, and that rewarded, through book reviewing and criticism, the achievement of a high level of production. Through constant application of standards of writing and illustrating, children's books improved and developed and grew in stature so that finally they were accorded recognition in the body of contemporary literature. Careful selection of books to use with children further emphasized the importance of their quality, as cheaper, mediocre books failed to find a place in collections designed for boys and girls.

As children's books became better in quality, the demand for them increased, and they began to be important in the economy of their publishers. Suddenly, they have become important in the economics of publishing. The publishing of children's books has become big business and has been taken over, often, by people who have little regard for their intrinsic value. Even children's books are subject to the practices of commercialism and are considered, too often, commodities for sale rather than books for children. As merchandise they take many forms: some are small, some large, some cost very little, and others are expensive; they are the rewritten classics, the adaptations, the splashy, shiny, highly colored gift books; the books designed to catch the eye of the unwary or to exploit the newest subject interest; they are for all ages and at all reading levels, and may tie in closely with curriculum emphases. Many of them appear as series books. Books published *en masse* or to catch the current fads may serve a purpose, but rarely possess the characteristics of permanent value that contribute to the development of taste, or that remain long with the child as a companionable memory. It is ironic that the very qualities that gave stature to children's books and earned for them a place in the world of literature are now being lost as they become more and more an item on a sales chart.

This development is not new. Rather, it is the extent to which it is increasing that is disturbing. In 1938 Anne Carrol Moore wrote in her "Three Owls" column in *The Horn Book Magazine*:

> The Owls have felt uneasy ever since the publication of children's books became profitable. There is grave danger lest American children's books become a commodity rather than a creative contribution to literature for children in all countries. . . . Integrities of the arts remain. It is the artist, the critic, the publisher and the public who are challenged and never, as it seems to me, has there been a more imperative call to defend our real treasures among children's books than in the year 1938.

With the substitution of 1960 for 1938, this criticism, this warning, is as applicable today as it was twenty years ago.

The one-of-a-kind, separate book is apt to be lost in the flood of quantity-produced and series books. Yet uniquely individual books are often the very ones that children will read and love if they can find them. These are the books that librarians would put in the basket. They are the ones that children's librarians must search out and identify, must shout about from the house tops, must provide for their young patrons in quantity. It would be easier to locate these books if they were separated from the mass-produced and series books, and could be evaluated in relation to other similar books. Books published in series have a ready-made audience, and children and children's librarians alike greet a new title in a familiar format with "Oh, here's another ———." Not so with a book written and published as an entity separate from and unlike any others. It must stand on its own merit and prove itself without previous introduction. This it can do, if it is good, but it must have time and opportunity, and when it is swamped by mass produced books there is little of either for it.

Early in the development of reading materials for children there was an acknowledgment of the differences in purpose and pattern between the text book and the trade book. Each had its place, its function, its standards, and the two kinds of books, without competing for attention, book funds, or in most instances authors, illustrators, or editors, supplemented each other and served the child. It is probably time now to consider a third category in literature for children, the series book. A considerable amount of the confusion and argumentation that accompanies any discussion of children's books grows out of the strong feeling that much of the material produced for children today can be classified neither as trade books nor as text books. Recognition of a third kind of book for children, with its own standards, patterns, and functions, would ease this bewilderment and give status to each of the three kinds of books. It would acknowledge that they are different, but in the acknowledgment would be acceptance of the idea that they *should* be different, each serving a recognized function in the provision of reading materials for children.

The unjust practice of holding series books to the standards for children's literature, and finding them wanting, would no longer obtain, but they would be judged by a different, more pertinent set of criteria. Eliminating the series books from consideration in the reviewing of trade books would keep the latter group more homogeneous and would result in a higher degree of critical evaluation. It may be noted that the other kind of book, the text book, influenced by the quality of trade books, has been undergoing steady improvement in text and illustration, while it retains its own characteristics and its undisputed place in the educative process.

There is room for many kinds of children's books so long as they are acceptable when evaluated by the standards which apply to them. Literate, reading children will discover them in great variety, especially the obvious, popular titles and books about subjects of current interest. Even these children need guidance, though, and the children's librarian points out for them the unusual, the hard to find, the special titles. There are still many of these which fill the basket to overflowing and, offered to the children, continue to delight them generation after generation.

FRANCES LANDER SPAIN

*Coordinator of
Children's Services*

They lived happily in his hut for a long time. . . .

The Contents of the Basket

Reflections on Children's Reading Here and in Japan

By Elizabeth Gray Vining

LAST SUMMER I heard Laurens Van der Post tell a story which has been fermenting in my mind ever since. He, as you know, is that very remarkable South African novelist, explorer, soldier and anthropologist, author of *Venture to the Interior* and *The Dark Eye in Africa* and other books, a wonderful combination of the man of action and the man of thought. The story which I am going to repeat for you now, not as he told it but as I remember it, was the first story that Laurens Van der Post remembers having heard, and it was told him by an old native servant on his grandfather's farm. A certain man in a little African village was charged with caring for the cattle that were the real wealth of the village. In the morning he milked them and took them to pasture, and in the evening he brought them back. One morning he found when he went to them that they had been milked during the night. The next day the same thing happened, and the next and the next. It was a serious loss for the village. He determined to stay up and watch the next night, to find out what was happening and if possible to catch the thief. So he hid behind a tree and waited.

In the moonlight he saw a band of people come down from the sky and milk the cattle. When he ran out they all fled, but he managed to catch and hold the last of them, a beautiful and shining maiden. He promptly fell in love with her and begged her to stay with him and become his wife. She consented, on the condition that he should never open the basket which she carried with her.

So they lived happily in his hut for a long time. The sky people did not come to molest the cattle and the village prospered. But all the time there stood in a corner of the hut that covered basket, to plague and tantalize the man. At length he could bear it no longer, and one day when his wife was out he opened it and looked inside. When she came back she knew at once what he had done and she charged him with it. He answered that yes, he had opened it and he could not see what all the fuss was about: there wasn't anything in the basket at all!

At that the sky maiden picked up her basket and went out of the house. Without looking back even once she walked steadily away until she was lost in the distance. She never came back.

The old servant who told Mr. Van der Post the story said to him, "It wasn't so much that he disobeyed and looked into the basket. That was human. The thing was, *he didn't see what was inside.* She couldn't forgive that."

The people who heard the story that night have various theories as to what was in the basket. My own interpretation is one that probably Mr. Van der Post would not recognize. It can of course be any value that some one cherishes, however invisible it may be to others. To me — though now I am milking Mr. Van der Post's cows — the basket is children's reading, and I am going to examine its contents with you this evening.

We who are here tonight have come together, at some expense of time and effort, because we care a great deal about children's reading. We know that it is important. We are concerned to get the best for our children.

There is a wealth of material from which to choose. Too much, actually, for when the presses grind out each year hundreds and hundreds of children's books, we know that they cannot all be good; no matter how fresh and bright and gay they look, the great mass of them are mediocre and it could not be otherwise. Faced with these mountains of bright volumes, we become confused, our choice — for we must choose — becomes haphazard. The libraries, public and school, perform an invaluable service for us not only in making available to our children the books which we cannot afford to buy but also in sorting and weeding out each year's production and culling the best.

Even so there is still a job to be done at home, and sometimes the richest homes do the poorest jobs. I think of some highly privileged boys I knew once who read nothing at all — nothing about people, or other countries, or the funny and amazing and wonderful things that happen — nothing but books that told them how to make or manage or play with their boats or model airplanes or whatever else was the craze of the moment. They had looked in the basket and all they found was jack-stones.

Sometimes when an object is too near or too complicated with detail to be seen clearly, it is a good idea to lay it aside and to look instead at a similar object, far enough away to be seen in perspective, and shorn of its ornaments so that we can see its essential elements. It may be interesting, then, to turn to Japan, where there are fewer children's books, where much less is thought and said about them, where libraries as we know them are comparatively rare, but where the children, like children everywhere, are eager and receptive.

Many Japanese children get their first introduction to literature through the Kamishibai Man, the modern equivalent of the old wandering story-teller. You will find him in any village, any city neighborhood that is off the main streets, down any crooked lane where there is room for fifteen or twenty children to gather. He claps two sticks together, ordinary square sticks that carpenters would call two-by-twos; they make a rather quiet but penetrating sound, and the children come running. He has a square wooden box about the size of an overnight case, and a tripod on which to set it up. Inside the box are big, gaily-colored cards with pictures on them. You can see the first card through the opening in the front of the box. Before he begins, however, he has a little business to do. He has some cheap candy to sell, and the ten-yen notes clutched in the fat little fists find their way into his pocket. Then he begins.

He tells the part of the story that goes with the first picture. That falls and the second picture comes up, carrying you on to the next development of the plot. The story-teller's memory is aided by the legend on the back of the card. The children see the pictures and they hear his voice. When the story reaches its climax, he may stop and sell some more candy, to catch the late-comers. I have seen them so many times as I went about Japan: the shabby man, the paper theater on its tripod, the crowd of red-cheeked, black-eyed, black-haired children, some in kimonos, some in knitted suits with ruffled aprons, always babies on the backs of the little girls — all absorbed and enthralled.

The quality of the story depends on the man and the kind of place from which he rents his material. It gives concern to thoughtful parents just as the comics and the TV serials do here. Some of them try to keep their children from listening, by refusing the ten-yen notes when they are begged for, but the same arguments prevail there as here: keeping the children quiet and occupied, the fact that all the other children do it, the natural desire to give what is wanted, the hope that some of the time there will be something worth listening to — and of course some of the time there is.

Three kinds of stories in general are told. Horror stories, stories of violence, terror, suspense, and so on are the easiest to attract a crowd with. Then there are the educational stories put out by serious-minded groups, Bible stories, moral tales, and so on, which suffer from the charge, as fatal as "Your slip is showing" — "Your message is showing." Then, and these are really the best loved, there are the traditional tales of Japan, as familiar to her children as Cinderella, the Three Bears, and Little Red Ridinghood are to ours. There is the story of the Tongue-cut Sparrow, in which the characters are faced, like Portia's suitors, with a choice among three baskets. The good old man humbly takes the smallest and finds in it gold and silver. The greedy old woman demands the largest and out of it jump witches and devils that pursue

her with clubs. There is the story of the man who for his devotion to a dog
was given the power of making flowers bloom on any bare branch that he
touched. There is the tale of the handsome young fisherman who visited the
palace at the bottom of the sea. There the princess fell in love with him and
gave him a lacquer box when he went home for a visit. He was, of course,
never to open the box, and, of course, he did. Smoke came out of it, envelop-
ing him and turning him into an old, old man, whose friends and relatives
had died a hundred years before and who could never find his way back to
the palace beneath the sea. A combination, as you see, of Pandora's box and
our African's basket and the Rip van Winkle theme. Aesop's Fables are also
a part of Japan's traditional tales, for the Portuguese brought them to Japan
in the sixteenth century, and those animal tales with their moral applica-
tions were so congenial to the thought of the country that they took root
there, and many Japanese are not aware that they were not a native growth.

But the Aesop Fables are more apt to appear in picture books than on the
Kamishibai Man's cards, because of their brevity.

The next stage is the picture books for small children that make up the
bulk of what is available for children. As I said before, the Japanese children
do not have the children's libraries that we have in such abundance. A library
movement has started and is growing, however, and not long ago I saw pictures of a bookmobile on the outskirts of Tokyo that looked just like our
county bookmobiles. But the Japanese child has something that our children
do not — the book store. There are far more bookstores in Japan than in the
United States and they are all open to children. There is not a tiny village or
a neighborhood shopping center in a city that has not at least one bookstore
and often more. They are small and simple, most of them, no more than a
room with one side open to the street, like a stage scene. Counters and shelves
run around three sides and in the center there are tables covered with books.
No heat and often no floor, just the pounded earth. There is always at least one
table spread with picture books and fringed with children eagerly reading.
Some of the readers are barely tall enough to breathe over the books. Some of
them can buy books but most do not; they simply come to read. The store-
keeper is always patient, even though he sees his stock getting shabby from
wear that brings him no return. The Japanese are wonderfully tender and
gentle with small children, and they are courteous to guests of any age,
even when uninvited. So the children read on undisturbed, and often their
parents buy what they clamor for.

I found the Japanese picture books entrancing, and I was there at a time
when paper was scarce and poor and they were done in the cheapest and

crudest way. They are mostly paper backs and not very thick, made to be sold for small sums, from ten to fifty cents in our money. They are ephemeral. An edition is printed and sold, the type destroyed. When the edition is gone, that is all. But there is a constant outpouring of vigorous, colorful, interesting picture books, with pictures that have life and originality and action. When they are done in the Japanese style, that is to say. There was an unfortunate tendency, when I was there, to copy Western illustration, and not the best but a static, chromo-like, second-rate Victorian sort of style. But those that were truly Japanese were full of sun and wind and rain and singing movement, all done with the utmost economy of line.

The traditional stories appear over and over, in longer and shorter versions, in all kinds of pictured interpretations. Then there are a great many picture books of a type that we scarcely have at all but which the children love. I mean the picture book that deals with the year's holidays. It begins with the New Year preparations and celebrations, the pounding of the rice — *petan, petan, petanko* — the decorations of pine and straw and lemon for the door, the dressing up of the family in their best kimonos, the little girls wearing clogs with bells in them, the visiting the shrine, the New Year's card game. Sometimes they are country children who celebrate, sometimes city children. Then follow the holidays in order, the Doll Festival, the Baptizing of the Baby Buddha in cherry-blossom time, the Boys' Festival, the Star Festival, the September shrine festivals, the harvest festival, and usually Christmas, from a strictly pagan point of view, with Santa Claus, reindeer, stockings, and Christmas trees. In one picture book I found what was evidently meant to be a generous inclusion of a Christian symbol: on the Christmas tree, beside the star, a crescent moon, and various toys was hung a cross!

There are extremely good nature picture books in beautiful color and with a touch of poetic feeling, showing flowers, birds, insects, shells, and the like.

There are many picture books that show child life in country villages, with the cycle of the rice planting, or in the mountains, with wood-cutting, charcoal burning, skiing, and sometimes mining. One thing that has always interested me is the impersonality of these books. There are always children, but no particular children. Even if there is a pair visiting their grandmother in the country and seeing many new sights, they are just a boy and a girl, not named, not individualized. In contrast I think of our picture books, where even a little tug in a harbor or a steam shovel has a name, a face, and a personality. It indicates, of course, two different approaches to life. In the West, we cherish the individual and his intrinsic worth and dignity. In the overcrowded East, only by sinking the individual in the mass can people manage to live in an orderly and peaceful way. It has been interesting to watch the change in Taro's Yashima books, written by a Japanese about Japanese children and published in this country for American children. The first two — *The Village Tree* and *Plenty to Watch* — both delightful and full of interest, were typically Japanese in that all the village children played in the tree or saw fascinating things on their way home from school. His third book, however, *Crow Boy*, is about a particular boy, a unique character with sorrows and victories. The book is wholly Japanese but it shows American influence.

There are plenty of picture books in Japan for the smallest children, but after that there is a dearth. For adolescents there is little to read unless they read translations, as they do, with enthusiasm. *Little Women* and *Little Lord Fauntleroy* are read more in Japan now, I should think, than in America. A book they love is Tolstoy's beautiful story, "What Men Live By." Most of my students knew that, having had it as children. They read Dickens and Hugo in translation, and *Quo Vadis* is a perennial. A number of my own books have been translated into Japanese and were very popular because they helped to fill a blank space. I was interested that *Sandy*, which is so definitely a girls' book here, was read by many Japanese boys. Some of them told me they liked it because it was cheerful and lively and they liked the freedom and initiative that the young people in the book enjoyed. Laura Ingalls Wilder's *Little House in the Big Woods* appeared while I was there and was immensely popular. Grown-ups read it as well as children, for the understanding of the United States that it gave them. Kanjiro Kawai, the famous potter, and a poet and a mystic as well, spoke of it to me with great appreciation. He was sensitive to the poetic quality of it, and he felt that it showed the pioneer spirit of America. How does that spirit manifest itself now, he wanted to know.

Through my teaching, in the two branches of the Peers School, I knew a good many Japanese boys and girls rather well. The hundred boys who were in the Crown Prince's class I taught for four years. Some of them came to my house one day a week besides to share in one of the Crown Prince's private lessons. I also taught classes in the Peeresses' school. Teaching English entirely *in* English as I did, it was essential that I find material interesting enough to make them want to talk. A routine of unconnected questions and answers was no good; sometimes I had to wait so long for the answer that I forgot the question. So I tried out a good many different devices and kinds of material in order to find the most effective. Through this means I learned the power of the story. I found that by telling them simply in English a story that really interested them and then discussing it afterwards, I could draw them into a real exchange of ideas, even though the medium of English was difficult for them. I soon learned which stories were most effective.

Short biographies, especially of people either living now or of recent memory, were always good. They wanted to know how other people managed their lives, people in other countries as well as their own. They were obviously matching their own ideals against those of others, trying on other lives for size, so to speak. One year we studied great men and women of the twentieth century. They chose five and I chose five, and we discussed their purpose in life, their difficulties, their achievements, their interests, their characters. At the end they said which were their favorites and why. I was impressed that those they chose were the ones they felt had made the greatest contribution to the world: Schweitzer, Helen Keller, Noguchi, Einstein, Madame Curie.

Even more than biographies, however, they were interested in stories that came from folklore, from legend, from myth. I made much use of a collection of tales which Sophia Fahs made, stories which illustrated the central theme, "Under the Sky All Men are One Family." She called it *Tales from Many Lands and Long Ago,* and she cast her net wide over all the continents and many of the nations. Another collection might have done as well, but this suited me perfectly, not only because of its theme but because of the short length and the variety of the stories, the clarity and simplicity with which they were told. Always there was an idea to take hold of, to examine and discuss.

One of the stories that opened up good discussion was "The Bell of Atri," which Longfellow used in his *Tales of a Wayside Inn.* You remember it: the king who hung a bell in the village so that all who felt unjustly used might ring it and obtain justice. The village in time was so well governed that the bell was never rung and a vine grew up over it. Then a poor old horse which was starved and beaten by its master ate the vine and rang the bell and awakened sleeping consciences.

There is, I have found since, a Japanese story that contains some of the same elements, but nobody told me about it at the time. I learned it in rather an odd way. When I left Japan one of the farewell gifts the Crown Prince gave me was a beautiful ornament on a lacquer stand, a drum, on which a silver cock was perched, and down below a silver hen and chick. When I asked the Crown Prince what it stood for, he was rather vague; the drum represented congratulations and good wishes, he said, and the cock had a sort of connection with him because he had been born in the year of the cock.

Last autumn, however, I was visiting the oriental collection in the Seattle Art Museum. The curator got out some very precious old *otsu-e*, the pictures that preceded the wood-block prints, and there on one of them was my drum and cock. The curator knew the story: an early emperor had given to his people a drum on which to beat when they felt unjustly treated. His reign, however, was so benign and just that the drum fell into disuse, and the barnyard cock climbed up on it to crow while the hen and chick played at the foot.

The same themes crop up again and again in the stories that people make up and tell to explain their lives, their experiences as a people, their aspirations, their sorrows, their fate: the bell and the drum that served justice, the forbidden basket, or apple, or lacquer box, the short sleep or visit that lasts a hundred years, the momentous choice. They may be stories of animals behaving like people, stories of gods, also like people, and heroes who are what we would like to be, while still retaining our more lovable faults. They may be told with grace and beauty, and when they are that is an added joy, or they may be stripped to their very bones. But still something living is left. There is vigor, honesty, courage, loyalty, a sensitiveness to inner "leading," a sense of mystery, a sense of justice — not legal, outward justice but inner, poetic justice, all that a child means when he cries out passionately, "That's not fair! "

We have a splendid variety of treasures in our basket of children's reading. Froth, too, of course, and chaff, but solidly tucked away for those who see are history, which helps us to estimate today in the frame of the past, books of adventure and exploration, fine novels written with distinction and understanding, which through vicarious experience lead their young readers into a deepening maturity, biography and nature lore and, perhaps best of all, poetry. I would not slight any of them, but especially, I hope, we will not be blind to those basic stories which have come out of the childhood of our race and have nourished the thoughts and hearts of countless generations of children. Rufus Jones, the Quaker philosopher and saint, said once that there was no better training for the imagination than the stories of Greek mythology, and William Ernest Hocking, for so long one of Harvard's great professors of philosophy, writes in his latest book, *The Coming World Civilization*, "The quiet molding of wills through the pictured decisions and characters of gods and heroes is empirically near-universal."

Endless entertainment and interest lie in these tales, but beyond that is the approach to the deep self, where symbols speak compellingly, and the imagination and the will are waiting to be stirred and fed.

Pastime and Happiness

The Family Reads Together

By ANNIS DUFF

VERY OFTEN on hearing of happy family reading experiences, people say how lucky the *children* are. And the children *are* lucky. No one, especially with the memory of his own childhood happiness with books, would deny that. But think how even luckier the parents are! For there can be few things more satisfying than seeing children take firm hold on something you know is going to be life-long resource and joy.

Most reading with children begins purely for the sake of amusing them, and if the whole thing stopped right there fathers and mothers would still be better off than when they started, because there's something so fortifying about being able to make a tiny person laugh. But once you've proved that something out of a book can turn that handsome trick, you're not likely to rest on your laurels. And it doesn't take long to make a discovery that's one of the best possible regulators of success in reading, not just to lap-sized children but with children of all ages. You find that there's lots more enjoyment for the listeners in something that you enjoy yourself. This is not to say, of course, that if you happen at the moment to be single-mindedly devoted to books about the deciphering of Hittite writings or the Dead Sea Scrolls that's the thing for bedtime reading with the little ones. One of the truly exciting privileges of living with new human beings is to be able, through them, to recover your own innocence of mind, to recapture your delight in the small things that form the basic texture of living. And this being the case, you strive for perceptiveness in choosing books that are not only immensely beguiling to you, but seem to please the baby of your heart.

Actually — and fortunately — you're not entirely dependent on your own embryonic perceptiveness. Generations of the soundest possible critics of children's literature have set the seal of approval on an enchanting array of the best possible books. The critics are the children, and the books are the books they've loved enough to keep them alive among the classics of literature.

Here you'll find Mother Goose's Nursery Rhymes, the oldest and dearest favorites of little childhood. To the happy youngsters who chuckle over *This Little Pig Went to Market* and *Humpty Dumpty* and *There Was an Old Woman Went up in a Basket,* they are jolly little games, or compact small stories, or things to wonder about; good strong simple, graphic words, and fine sturdy rhythms. To the grownup who repeats them from memory, or reads them from a book with beautiful pictures — Leslie Brooke's *Ring O' Roses* or Kathleen Line's *Lavender's Blue* are two of the loveliest — they are a renewal of friendship with literature so old that no one knows any more where some of it came from. Some of Mother Goose's rhymes have historical significance that means nothing to the inexperienced minds of little children but has a genuine fascination for the adult who's interested in such things. I remember my own extra pleasure in saying "rub-a-dub-dub" — with actions — to a small boy, because of having learned that it originated at the time of the Reformation in Scotland. Church bells were forbidden as "smacking of Popery" in calling people to worship, and instead drums were beaten — "rub-a-dub-dub." The "tub" refers to the round, walled pulpit usual in Scots churches, and the "three men" — the butcher, the baker, the candlestick maker — represent the lay preachers who held forth where formerly only vested ministers had stood. And "they all put to sea in a rotten potato" is a reference to the terrible famine of those years caused by potato blight. That's only one of the political broadsides of former times that little children have taken to their hearts and invested with their own meanings.

Not all of Mother Goose has any specific meaning to either child or grownup, but the overtones of true poetry are there, inviting the imagination, by words and images, to construe meanings that satisfy the feelings.

> I had a little nut-tree,
> Nothing would it bear
> But a silver nut-meg
> And a golden pear.
>
> The King of Spain's daughter
> Came to visit me
> And all for the love
> Of my little nut tree.
>
> I skipped over ocean
> I danced over sea
> And all the birds
> In the air
> Couldn't catch me.

Even more elusive and lovely is the ancient spring song which begins

> Here we come a-piping
> In springtime and in May,
> Green fruit a-ripening
> And winter fled away.

Many of the stories little children love the best are part of the same ancient tradition. *Goldilocks and the Three Bears* is one — a reliable favorite — and *The Old Woman and Her Pig, Three Little Pigs, The Gingerbread Man*. All of these and dozens more are compounded of the same imperishable elements that make all good literature — genuine ideas, good, simple, sturdy language, honest presentation of character where character is involved, and the quality of honest creation that is so difficult to define but so easy to identify in contrast with what is merely manufactured.

These elements are present in the best of the books that have been created for little children in modern times — *Johnny Crow's Garden*, for instance, and *The Story about Ping, Millions of Cats, A Walk in the Forest*, and Marie Hall Ets' most enchanting book, *Play with Me*. The wonderful thing about these newer books is the way artists have used their best gifts to make pictures that go hand in hand with the words to achieve the maximum of action and fun and beauty. Fathers and mothers who are just beginning their careers as companions-in-reading with small fry may sometimes find themselves a little bewildered by the very lavishness of illustration, the variety of styles, the profusion of color. But here again is a delightful experience in store, of recapturing the purity of a child's way of seeing things, and at the same time of learning perhaps for the first time what it is that makes a picture really good for what it's intended to do.

Not very long ago at a meeting of teachers one of them said, "I don't quite understand why it's so important to try to find the *best* books for little children. Do they know the difference?" The answer to such a question seems fairly obvious. Maybe little children don't know the difference at first. But they can learn. And when you think that the impressions of childhood go the deepest and last the longest, doesn't it seem only fair to make the first experiences with books not only as blissful as can possibly be, but also *worth remembering?*

There's this to think about too: what little people learn in these more impressionable years, before their minds become cluttered and confused in the great wide world outside their homes, can be the beginning of good, reliable standards of taste and judgment. Then too, where the enjoyment of people of assorted ages is concerned, as it is in family reading, there's simply got to be substance in the books you read together. It's only in good books, with *real* stories, *real* imagination, *real* people, *real* fun, that you find the substance of present delight and future good memories.

I don't mean to suggest that families can't have good times reading just run-of-the-mill books. Especially if for some reason not quite apparent to the elders a younger member takes a fancy to some particular book of no great merit, it would be pretty stuffy not to make room for it in the family circle. Often rather mediocre books can lead the way into better ones. I'm not sure that our family doesn't owe it to Enid Blyton that Arthur Ransome came into favor with our son earlier than he might have done otherwise. It happened when he was about seven and somebody presented him with one of those Adventure books — you know, *Castle of —, Cave of—, Ship of —,* I can't remember which. Anyway, we read it en famille because the boy wasn't yet quite able to manage it on his own. And it wasn't at all bad fun, really — the conversation of the youngsters is often very brisk and amusing. My husband and I got pretty bored before the end — but not before we'd realized that it was the idea of a gang of children having adventures by themselves that appealed so strongly to both of our children. It was my turn to choose the next book for reading aloud and just on the off-chance that it wouldn't be beyond our young man's enjoyment, I chose *Swallows and Amazons.* And was I the popular mother! Even though the young man is now almost completely grownup he still occasionally reads the Ransome stories with delight because they are *good.*

This points up another feature of reading with children. It's probably a common experience with parents to find that a youngster who only yesterday, it seemed, was perfectly happy with the bookish amusement you provided for him, today is a young person of very definite individual interests and curiosities. And finding books to satify those intensely individual preferences is a perfectly delightful way for fathers and mothers to explore and understand the personality of a unique human being.

From the point of view of shared reading, it's necessary to find a least common denominator of interest, so to speak, for children of varied ages and temperaments, because of course no one member's interests should dominate. It wouldn't be fun that way — although later on when children reach the stage of making their own discoveries among books there's a special kind of fun in the way the whole family can be swept into enthusiasm for one discoverer's favorites.

But what everybody just naturally loves to share at any stage is laughter. And from the nursery age on, books of really good nonsense are just about the finest equipment any household can have. Now that both of our children have come to the point of reminiscing about their childhood it's absolutely soul-satisfying to hear them say, "Oh, and do you remember how we laughed over *Timothy Turtle?*" — or maybe it's *Giant Otto* or *Homer Price* or *Pippi Longstocking.* And then we start laughing all over again, and as likely as not get out the books and re-read them. It's marvelous to find how well they wear, and good to be reminded that learning to laugh again, in the specially free and hearty way that children laugh, is one of the best gifts that parenthood brings.

Learning to ask questions and to feel a real tingle of excitement in finding answers is another of the blessings fathers and mothers often owe to their children. For it's woefully easy for minds occupied with the cares and responsibilities of adult living to lose both their effervescent curiosities, and the resilience of memory that preserves the harvest of answers those curiosities bring.

Maybe a small boy finds an arrowhead in his own garden, and asks how it came there, and who dropped it? And when? And why? You probably don't know the answers. But it's splendid fun to make a trip to the library to look for them. You may start with a simple book for a simple little boy, and find five years later that he's still pursuing his interest in, for instance, Elizabeth Chesley Baity's *Americans Before Columbus* — which possibly teaches you incidentally more than you ever knew before! Maybe a little girl wants to know the name of a big blue star that hangs above the fading summer sunset. You know it's Venus, but that's about all. So you look it up, perhaps in Peter Lum's *The Stars in Our Heaven*, if that's what happens to be handy. And first thing you know you're deep in the fascination of stars, planets and constellations, and the lovely myths and legends that explain their names. Who knows, a long time afterward the interest that began with one star may be the basis for understanding of, and deep delight in, such a book as Fred Hoyle's *The Nature of the Universe*. The intangible benefits of knowing that children's good minds are growing in strength and reach by being fed are beyond price.

Perhaps even more far-reaching are the benefits of stimulating and feeding the imagination of the young. The other morning my daughter and I were hanging the laundry in the garden when she suddenly startled me by saying, "Hi, Timmy Tiptoes, haven't you had enough trouble from digging up other people's nuts?" I looked over and there was a fat gray squirrel in the flower bed — I suspect digging for my crocus bulbs. We talked to him for a minute or two and then went on talking to each other about Beatrix Potter and what pure delight her books have given us. After a few moments of thoughtful silence my daughter said, "I wonder if modern children have imaginary friends and imaginary adventures from watching television the way we did from reading books?" I wonder too. I wonder if there's any such stimulus for children in a visual experience as there is in knowing all the wonderful old folk and fairy tales like *The Twelve Dancing Princesses* and *The King of Ireland's Son;* the stories of gods and heroes like King Arthur and Odysseus; all the superlative modern creations of fancy like *At the Back of the North Wind* and *Martin Pippin in the Daisy Field,* and *The Borrowers?* It seems to me that in a world so full of cruelty and destruction as this we need the spiritual grace and stability that can come only through imagination. Our children are the ones who can help us to find this, and keep it.

Poetry shared with children has something of the same revivifying influence. Children whose ears are tuned in their early listening days to the cadence of poetry are likely to come in time, by way of A. A. Milne, and Robert Louis Stevenson, and Christina Rossetti, to appreciation of such as William Blake and John Milton and William Shakespeare. Poetry by its very nature is remarkable and much that is delightful just to listen to has meaning that grows with the growing person.

*   *   *

I know that many fathers and mothers feel they have neither the time nor the money to spend on reading with their children. But spending time with children is a way of living with children that's awfully good for the people who have them, as well as for the children themselves. And there aren't many cosier ways of being together than with books that everybody enjoys. Reading leads to such splendid talks! Of the families who do make of their reading together a real exercise in companionship there are probably no two who will do it in quite the same way.

But I should think there could be few fathers and mothers experienced in sharing their own pleasure in reading fully and honestly and joyfully with their children who would not feel in their bones what fine and enduring benefits come from it — benefits of learning together what the constant mind of man, in all times and states of being, has recorded in words on paper for the pleasure and comfort and stimulus and growth of people in all times to come.

I should think there must be few people who can look back on their own childhood joy in reading, treasure the renewed delight of sharing books with *their* children, look forward eagerly and hopefully — as I do — to carrying on a tradition of delight with grandchildren, who would not recognize the shining truth of the words

> Dreams, books, are each a world; and books, we know,
> Are a substantial world, both pure and good.
> Round these, with tendrils strong as flesh and blood,
> Our pastime and our happiness will grow.

The Hero's Changing Face

By Elizabeth Enright

TODAY I am going to talk about the changing fashions — the changing tastes — in the heroes and heroines of children's fiction. Since these fashions and tastes are always imposed by adults, perhaps it would have been more appropriate to call this talk "The Crib of Procrustes."

Juvenile writing, like every other, and moreover like all arts, crafts, styles in furniture or clothes or manners, is a product of its times, and therefore adds its little share to the world's history. Heroes and heroines of children's books, like heroes and heroines of adult novels, are the offspring of minds, attitudes, opinions, formed in the prevailing spirit of the day. Though a few of us are rebels, nearly all the rest of us are guided by the modes of culture of our era

In the beginning, of course, there was Once upon a Time. In the beginning there were what we call the fairy-tales, which, though they rarely contained accounts of fairies, always contained magic. These tales which had their roots in earliest mythology and legend — in fact in the earliest expressions of man's imagination — were never, in the beginning, intended as stories for children. At least not for children only. They were, I suppose, meant for the entire family; the entire community.

In these stories the number 3 was of the greatest significance: three wishes, three sons, three crowns, three chances at opportunity; and the cast presented in the story usually numbered three, too: three characters who were symbols: the princess, absolutely good and beautiful; the prince, absolutely brave and handsome; the witch or the ogre or the stepmother, who was absolutely evil and destructive.

So the first three faces that appeared in the stories wore the masks of beauty, of fortitude, and of evil.

These three had no real personalities, there was nothing in them — no complexity of character or human foible — to puzzle or disconcert the listener. The prince was wholly deserving of the stout material rewards he was granted at the end of his trials (halves of kingdoms, the hand of the princess, the castle, or the coffer of jewels). As for the princess, all that was required of her was to be beautiful and have golden hair; for these reasons, naturally, she was granted everything. And as for the wicked witch she was wholly deserving of her hideous punishment. Luckily we were never encouraged to feel pity for her: she was properly made to dance in red-hot iron shoes till she fell dead, or she was nailed in a barrel and rolled downhill into the river. Now and then, to vary the pattern, two ravens might fly down out of the air to pluck her eyes out.

I am speaking now of the fairy-tales that were the archetypes, such as those of the Brothers Grimm (and grim they were in their original state). We could go on and talk about the more sophisticated stories by Perrault (who invented Cinderella) or the lovely melancholy fantasies of Hans Christian Andersen, but I prefer the Grimms' tales and their prototypes from other lands for illustration since they had their roots in the rugged soil of folklore.

Now besides those three principal characters of the fairytale there was something else, another character, really; for magic was in itself a character, magic was the air that talked, giving advice or geographical directions to the hero or heroine. It was the dragon that clanked and glittered on the palace stair; it was the harp that sang, or the magic carpet, or the genie. And I believe it may be because of this character of magic that the fairy-tales have more or less fallen into disfavour. Certainly it is true that children no longer read them as avidly as they used to; parents no longer encourage them to as they once did. And why is this?

I have a theory that we have lost our taste for magic because we have, in many cases, made it come true. We've worked and toiled to wrest the cloudy symbols out of the imagination and convert them into objects you can buy in a store. Or use in a war.

Voices do speak out of the air. There is a wonderbox that shows us visions. Our version of the magic carpet travels across every sky carrying its load of commercial travelers, elderly relatives, or bags of mail; and if the cow has not yet jumped over the moon, the little dog who laughed to see such sport has already circled the earth a great number of times. As for the dragons, they are positively commonplace; they stutter and racket in the farmers' fields, hoot through every city street, and bellow their fire across the battlefields. Dragons are everywhere.

And we are very familiar with the genie by now. He's come out of his bottle, and is as tall as the sky: he wears a domeshaped cap of clouds. We are in the position of the poor fisherman: we still don't know whether we've released a slave or a destroyer.

So we have discovered that magic, once persuaded from its legend into reality, is a mixed blessing, and like the magic in the fairy-tale may well have the last word. It is not a cozy commodity. And so, for this reason we have, a little, lost our taste for the fairy-tale that first described it.

But now let us leave magic and the early tales and go on to the more realistic stories, for and about children, that first began to make their appearance in the eighteenth century. Rousseau, Oliver Goldsmith, and John Newbery of England were all partly responsible for the development of this kind of fiction; so it is really only in the past two hundred years that there have been stories written particularly and especially for children.

First of all — thanks largely to Rousseau — there were the didactic story-tellers. Most of them were women: Mrs. Trimmer, Mrs. Barbauld, Mrs. Sherwood, and above all, Mrs. Edgeworth. These ladies, as one reads their works, emerge as formidable figures: laced and boned and petticoated, they bristled and bustled and clacked their tongues. They pounced on mischief like great she-eagles, and glared like gorgons in search of misdemeanors; and if they ever smiled — at least in their prose — it was a very frosty smile; and if they ever laughed it was with a tone of moral disparagement.

Their attitude can best be summarized in their own words.

Mrs. Sherwood wrote as follows:

> All children are by nature evil, and while they have none but the evil principle to guide them, pious and prudent parents must check their naughty passions in any way that they may have in their power and force them into decent and proper behaviour.

Mrs. Trimmer contributed this:

> The rod is the very best thing to apply
> When children are crying and cannot tell why.

These women — one is tempted to call them "didactresses" — earnestly believed that they knew all the rules and that the child could be espaliered on them like a young tree.

I suppose that in their own homes they must have been human; most of them were mothers, and as mothers they must have been subject to all the tenderness, exasperation, and delight known to mothers in general; but it's hard to believe it when you read their works. They were never afraid — as we are now — to use horror or gloom as a weapon for reform.

Mrs. Trimmer was fond of writing little fables in rhyme, each of which taught a lesson. Among them is one about little Jane and Tom who were foolish enough to eat some red berries they found in a lane. It goes like this:

> But long they had not been at home
> Before poor Jane and little Tom
> Were taken, sick and ill, to bed,
> And since, I've heard, they both are dead.
> Alas! Had Tommy understood
> That fruit in lanes is seldom good
> He might have walked with little Jane
> Again along the shady lane.

Didacticism was the keynote of all these books: entertainment as such was not the object: it was the sugar coating for the bitter pill of instruction and reform. Every time a child strolled across a meadow, looked into a shop window, wondered at the constellations on the night sky, there was an adult close at hand — a parent, usually — to inform and preach a moral.

Mrs. Edgeworth's famous tale of *Rosamund and the Purple Jar* is an example. Rosamund and her mother have started out to buy Rosamund a pair of new shoes. On their way they pass an apothecary shop, and the little girl is fascinated by a large ornamental purple jar in the window. She insists that she would rather have this than the new shoes, and her mother, after offering every objection except the right one, which is to *tell* the child the jar is nothing but plain glass filled with colored water, allows her to purchase it. Rosamund is soon disillusioned, and is further disappointed by being denied an excursion with her father because he is mortfied by the lamentable condition of her shoes.

The popularity — for generations — of this story is explained by the fact that Rosamund is a very human little girl. Her mother, however, is one of the most detestable women in fiction. (*Why* didn't she explain about the jar? And why did she allow the child's shoes to reach such a condition in the first place?)

Parents were horrors in those days. Consider Mr. Fairchild of *The Fairchild Family*, who took his children, after a hearty dinner, to look at the weatherbeaten corpse of a murderer hanging from a gallows' tree, in order to emphasize the fact that it's a dangerous thing to quarrel.

(In this connection, I wonder if it is not these fictional parents of the didactic era that have caused the widespread revulsion against parents in children's books — at least in books for older children. For, since that era, parents have been more or less relegated to the background; and often they are killed off before the action begins at all. The ways of getting rid of them are varied: shipwrecks, cholera, automobile accidents; and in recent years, one authority tells me, the plane crash has taken a heavy toll of fictional parents. In my own case I have found the extensive lecture trip or business in Europe useful.)

As the Victorian era got its teeth into English and American culture, the style of heroes in children's books began to undergo a change. Whereas in the days of Mrs. Trimmer the young characters had been naughty and in need of strict training and informing, they had at least been healthy. But now the heroes and heroines of a later day were, while alarmingly good and pious, usually in a state of precarious health.

An early death was highly desirable in the fiction of this era. The specific nature of the fatal malady was seldom made clear, though a process called "wasting" was universally popular and in frequent use. Sunlight played on aureoles of golden hair; and violet eyes, lash-fringed, were fixed on heaven. Often the little sufferer was musically inclined, the violin falling from the senseless grasp on the last page. Before the end, however, he had always brought to rectitude the evil-doer, and those in rude health who stood about the sick-bed drenched in tears of grief and admiration. The final chapter was reserved to point a moral so obvious and oppressive that often the reader had been smoked out of the story before the end.

These were the days of Elsie Dinsmore who wept and fainted her way through 26 volumes (if you didn't die you could at least faint). Elsie had a worldly father whom she was able to wear down to a state of submission and repentance by the simple method of keeling over or bursting into a flood of tears when crossed. One's heart yearns over Mr. Dinsmore. (The Dinsmore books were the only books denied my mother by my grandmother, so she bootlegged them from the library until she proved to herself that they were insufferable.)

It's pretty safe to guess that no true human being ever behaved like the afflicted characters in these stories, but no doubt there were horrible infants who thought it fashionable to try. One's heart yearns over *their* parents, too!

Fortunately, this era of deathbeds and swooning and tears did produce some voices that were vital and original. There was Lewis Carroll, for instance, and George McDonald; and in America there was Louisa May Alcott, who proved once and for all that the children of the era were actually human beings. She had a true ear; her characters lived and were beloved, and I should think the discovery of them must have come as a tremendous relief to all those children who had been pounded over the head with morals, and incited to weep as often as possible, by other authors.

But Louisa Alcott was, after all, a product of her day, and the most virtuous character in her most famous book was made to undergo the "wasting" process, finally laying down her needle because she said it was "too heavy," and then, of course, dying.

However, as time went on the process again began to change. Dying was a little passé, but ill health continued to be highly thought of. The invalid persisted, but this time with a difference: he or she was allowed to recover. The hero, or heroine, usually started out as a rebellious and reckless tomboy and pretty soon he managed to break his back or his neck or something, and came to courage and manliness — or grace and womanliness — through long

months or years (preferably years) of suffering. To me and others like me
the hero was never as interesting after the treatment as before and we care-
lessly skipped over all those conversational exchanges with Cousin Helen or
kindly Uncle Fred in which the hero was brought to the realization that All
was for the Best, et cetera.

In fact when we read those old books we scanned every passage of dialogue
with a suspicious eye, appraising it for moral content, and then skipping.

Then, toward the end of the wheel-chair era, and despite the great authors
of children's stories who began to emerge (Mark Twain, Robert Louis Stevenson, Howard Pyle, Kipling, and so on), another trend began to be apparent.

About the turn of the century the invalid, though still on deck, began to
be somewhat neglected in favor of the Poor Child or the Poor Family. (The
most popular stories included both: poverty and ill-health.)

The Poor Child and the Poor Family had one reward in common: sooner
or later they were befriended, often adopted, by a wealthy bachelor or
widower who owned a limousine and a great house on a hill, filled with fur
rugs and mastiffs and Tiffany glass.

It's curious that the benefactor was almost without exception a male, and
an unattached male at that. Very often he was crusty and despondent; his
hard wounded heart had to be thawed out gradually, page after page, by
the artless prattling of his charge or charges.

It's queer, too, that the benefactor, while single and Older, rarely married
the widowed mother of the family. Sometimes he waited until the eldest
daughter or the befriended orphan reached the age of consent, and then he
married her. Oftener than not it was enough for him to play the role of
Father-substitute; to lean back in his Morris chair, as the eldest daughter
played Mendelssohn on the piano, and his fingers toyed with the curls of
the youngest daughter seated on the floor beside him prattling comments
of baby wisdom (all spelled out in baby-talk). The boys, if there were any,
were always quiet and probably clean, the mastiffs never barked or scratched
at fleas, and the widowed mother, now relegated to the role of dignified house-
keeper, sat somewhere to one side, usually mending and smiling quietly.
Everybody was beautifully dressed except the mother and she was decently
dressed. She was entirely beyond vanity or thoughts of Self.

Rewards in the era of the Wealthy Benefactor were always material, and
lovingly catalogued by the authors. (Books of the genre are *The Five Little
Peppers, Sara Crewe, Little Lord Fauntleroy, Rebecca of Sunnybrook Farm.*)

It's worth noting that even in the Horatio Alger books the hero usually
rose to his splendid financial heights through the interest and good offices

of a wealthy gentleman. Of course he had to be a good, virtuous boy. In those days, in fiction, if you were good, modest, and industrious, somebody was certain to come along and reward you by seeing that you got rich.

These stories about Male Benefactors were, of course, one outgrowth of a materialistic era, an era of amassing fortunes. It was, above all, a man's era. He roamed in a paradise of Free Enterprise where there was as yet no Women's Suffrage, no world war, no taxes. There was nothing but the needling of his conscience to jab him in the direction of philanthropy. Titans stalked the land with a firm grip on the moneybags; and some of them were generous. In the fantasies there was *always* one who was generous.

But then came the first fearful thunderclap. For our country, at least, and certainly for the Titans, it had been a long, sunny picnic in the fields, and it was a shock of the first magnitude to discover that civilization was as subject to storms and disasters and upheavals as the planet itself.

This shock and the struggle of readjustment had their effect on everything; even on the sort of children's books that now began to rise in popularity. One phenomenon was the story of manic optimism: Pollyanna, for instance, and Georgina of the Rainbows. These two heroines were girls who contrived not only to make silk purses out of sows' ears, but silk purses with silver linings out of sows' ears! Everything was grist to their inflexible cheer.

They, and several others like them, lived on into the 1920s, but as far as I can ascertain, were finally left stranded and drying in the low tide of the 1930s.

During the Depression the trend does not seem to have been so clear, perhaps because nothing was clear. There was a resurgence of the fairy-tale fantasy, I remember, a great number of books about the children of other countries, and here and there stories with a strong proletarian flavor. I contributed one myself about a healthy farm child.

And after the Depression came the next war and the next; all the major events of our era as adults. And since we are in the middle of it we cannot see our own trend very distinctly. We can see those of the past — one overlapping the other, always, and even merging with it — but each still fairly well defined as a trend.

Already, however, one cultural characteristic of our era *is* apparent in certain books for the very young. These deal with familiar facts. Johnny and Betsy go to the supermarket with Mommy. Bobby goes to nursery school for the first time and Mommy stays with him till he feels secure. Nancy is encouraged to give her doll a bath while Mommy bathes the sibling. All these stories have a sort of antiseptic coziness. Mommy glows with permissiveness and if you stuck a pin into her she wouldn't yell.

These are books for the littlest ones, and though one may mock them it is probably true that what motivates them is what motivates those that *we* write for the older, middle group, of children.

A child's book, in my opinion, is compounded of two prime ingredients: wish and memory. The wishes are often those that have lain forgotten in our minds since we were children; wishes that we had as children. And the memories are also from our childhood; they rise up involuntarily, often surprising us, when we begin to write if we write truly.

But to those wishes which were only for ourselves others are added now: wishes for the people who are children today.

What can we promise them? Security? No, we cannot promise them that; now less than ever. The factory-magic we've contrived threatens them as it does us.

Happiness? How happy is this world? How can we promise them a thing like that!

But we *can* wish these things for them, and hope them and depict them, so that the child who *enters* a book in a way no adult can, finds himself in a world which, though it may contain trial and conflict, also reveals security and reason and humor and a good measure of happiness.

And so, finally, to the gallery of faces: the blank sweet face of the princess, the stern little faces of the didactic children, the saintly smile of the Victorian invalid, and the relentless grin of the Pollyannas, we can now add the face we have tried to devise for the children of our own era: a face that is fairly familiar, possibly dirty, but healthy and reasonable; above all a hopeful face.

Animal History will Bear this Out

By WILLIAM PÈNE DU BOIS

I T is indeed an honor to be invited to speak on such an illustrious occasion as this fiftieth anniversary. This is also somewhat of an anniversary for me. Exactly twenty years ago today I was invited to speak right here in this same room at a similar but younger meeting, but fortunately for those present, I never quite reached the podium. It was a cold day and an icy breeze was blowing up and down Forty-Second Street. But in this exact same room it was frightfully warm, and the steam radiators were banging away at a fearful pace.

Miss Anne Carroll Moore and I were strangers at the time, and as I entered the room she directed me to a seat in the rear, near a window, and instructed me to either open or shut the window and demonstrated a discrete signal which was to serve as cue. This worked out nicely and I well remember an address by Doctor Seuss about some rather extraordinary doings on Mulberry Street. The system worked well until Miss Moore herself made a delightful address in the success of which she absently flashed our secret signal seventeen times in one exciting minute, and the poor window became a guillotine in the heat of the revolution. She told me rather firmly to sit down and stay down, and then finished her talk by saying something to the effect that, "William Pène du Bois was supposed to be here to speak, but has apparently been blown off the streets by the stiff winds outside."

I heaved a sigh of tremendous relief, but some traitor in the audience (who turned out to be my publisher, May Massee) said that I had been there all the time, and pointed to me before I had a chance to duck behind the chairs. Knowing that I couldn't possibly follow up two such delightful talks (and now that I look back at it what I had planned to say was very odd indeed) and being scared to death anyway, and feeling that the best air-conditioners are those which make the least noise while operating, I flatly refused to speak; and the party broke up cheerfully and the guests departed wreathed in smiles. But I do remember that on my way out a lady of vast proportions grabbed me by the lapels and shook me like a puppy. "Listen here young man," she said, "the next time you're asked to speak, YOU SPEAK!" I promised that I would, and here I am, but I will confess that I still shake at the thought of speaking, and the mere suggestion that I address an audience sends me, as the old saying goes, running to the nearest window.

But since that day I treasure my friendship with Anne Carroll Moore, and I feel that it is indeed nice to have someone think back of you as being in some way related to a breath of fresh air.

And why this fear of talking? It's simply that there are some artists and writers who talk a great deal about their work and others who never mention it at all, and in more general terms there are people who talk a great deal and others who are quite silent, and then too there are participators and spectators. I fall into the second of these three sets of categories — I'm a very silent spectator.

Now what does a silent spectator talk about when cornered? Well since I've hardly used the medium at all, the possibilities are immense, spread out all over this and more imaginative planets, and since I've only made one other talk in my whole life, the chances of my repeating myself are remote. So I'll be trite and banal and try to answer the first question I'm always asked about a book, and I'm sure all other writers are asked first — which is, "How did you ever think of such a crazy idea?" And to illustrate my answer I shall discuss a short book of mine named *Lion*.

Usually when asked this question, "How did you ever think of such a crazy idea?" being a silent-spectator type, I give a quick answer which over a period of twenty years has been burnished and refined to the following words: "I take a hot hot bath and some time between the slow rising of billowy clouds of steam, and the slow descent of drops of water on the tile walls there emerges an idea for a children's book." I find this answer puts an end to the conversation generally, but it's not quite long enough for this distinguished podium. I once illustrated some travel journals by Somerset Maugham in which he described smoking opium and said the effects were quite similar to the blissful state which overcomes one after soaking for hours in a very hot tub when one becomes quite overcome with wild flights of imagination. This seems to me a rather British description of a romantic Oriental pastime, but I seem to detect perhaps his giving away of a secret which I hitherto thought was all mine, and now that the cat is out of the bag, I wouldn't be in the least surprised if the world were soon to see a whole new generation of well-scrubbed writers. And now back to *Lion*.

The plot of *Lion* is extremely simple. The foreman of an Animal Factory in Heaven where animals are being designed for the purpose of populating the various planets of the Universe thinks of a name for an animal and that name is LION.

The name LION seems so good to him that he decides to design the animal to go with it himself. He hasn't done any actual designing since he was a very young boy and drew a wiggly line with a brown crayon which he named WORM. For designing WORM, a highly functional multi-purpose animal, he received a medal and was made foreman of the factory. (He wasn't literally made "foreman," he was put in charge — his name was Foreman and the job as we've come to know it was named after him.)

Well, not having designed an animal in years, centuries perhaps, he is a bit out of practice and unsure of himself. His first design for LION is a small multi-colored bug with a fur body, a head trimmed with feathers and the tail of a fish. Not feeling too sure of this design, he puts the same question to six of his assistants, and this question is, "TELL ME IN ONE WORD WHAT IS WRONG WITH THE LION." As boss, he doesn't feel like hearing a more lengthy criticism from his underlings.

The answers come back in one word each: "SIZE," "FEATHERS," "COLOR," "LEGS," "HAIRCUT," and finally that one marvelous answer he's been waiting for, "*NOTHING!*" and the KING OF BEASTS has been designed!

That's all there is to the story.

Now don't get me wrong, no hot hot bath was wasted on that little plot alone. No. Up to this point I haven't set foot in a tub. The year before I wrote *Lion*, I received a Christmas card from a cousin of mine, a good artist named Margot Tomes, and she had drawn a lion who was gently and quietly perusing Jesus in the manger, a sweet smile on his furry face. This lion was beautiful except that he had legs which were a bit thin. My cousin has a poodle trimmed like a lion and the influence must have been a bit overpowering. I wrote her telling her how much I loved the card and then said that if I were asked to tell in one word what was wrong with the lion, I would answer "LEGS." This in itself was most rude, because I wasn't asked and my cousin and I detest criticism from each other in any shape or form. Well, that Christmas card brought forth the plot, so now on to the baths.

What does an Animal Factory in Heaven look like? That took a bit of soaking. I first decided that it should be off by itself, a unit apart, in the suburbs of Heaven. Then came the question of gravity — is there gravity in Heaven? Of course not! God invented gravity to keep things put as he placed them on other planets. There is no need for gravity in Heaven. Angels have wings so they can keep their hands free as they go up, down, sideways, across, playing lutes, flutes and oboes. But for sitting at a drawing table, and I'm thinking with partiality based on my own experience, I reasoned that there should be a slight force of gravity to hold things in place such as pots of paint and boxes of crayons. So I placed the Animal Factory on a magnetic platform. This created a danger to the younger, smaller, angels with little wings, a danger of being drawn abruptly to the platform and stuck there as on fly paper, so I placed a raised platform, high above the factory, a platform on which to land which was connected to the factory by a very long slide. Up there the gravitational pull would be quite mild — just enough to slide an angel down gently into the factory itself.

What kind of power should be used to make animals? I suppose atomic power would be truest, but I thought steam would be warmer so I borrowed a magnificent steam engine from F. A. O. Schwarz Toy Store and used that familiar machine to make the Animal Factory look like a factory. Actually if one is really creative no mechanical power is needed at all.

The buildings themselves were made from materials on hand such as fur, feathers, and fish scales. There were two badminton courts for exercise during lunch hour. Badminton was invented at the Animal Factory, the rackets being strung with leftover cat gut, and the birds made with bits of leftover leather and feathers.

There is a drawing in *Lion* of angels flying to the Factory drawn by kites. This isn't a mode of celestial transportation, far from it! Flying without gravity takes no effort whatsoever. The angels with the kites are testing new designs of frameworks for birds. The kite, another Animal Factory invention, obviously came before the bird; and then, billions of years later poor man had to start with the bird and go backwards through the kite to arrive at *his* flying machine.

I decided that there should be no color in Heaven, only black and white — color being a frivolous device for the amusement and camouflage of lesser planets.

Just one more thing. It says in the book that there were one hundred and four artists who sat on silver stools behind one hundred and four white wooden tables. The studio was actually quite like a classroom.

They sat in twenty-six rows of four angels each, alphabetically: four A's in the first row, four B's in the second, four C's in the third and so forth; and like a classroom, the bright angels sat in the front rows and the dunces in the back rows.

Animal history will bear this out.

Imagine for instance this front row, the A row, in which the four angels are designing animals which begin with letter "A."

The first angel is designing that most delicate, industrious and well organized of all animals, the wondrous ant; while sitting next to him, a brilliant and witty angel is designing the clever and imaginative aardvark to eat the ants his meticulous comrade is creating.

The third angel is designing the swift, elegant, graceful antelope — a beautiful bit of thinking, while his crafty neighbor, the forth angel has up his creative sleeve an ingenious snare to catch this speedy animal at the watering hole, the fearsome trap-jawed alligator.

Yes, four brilliant minds at work in row A.

Now, walk back to the rear of the room and consult the dunces. In row Y some waggish dolt is working on the Yak which he obviously cribbed from the Ox in row O — while in row Z an even lazier angel is leaning over his shoulder and copying the Yak and calling it a Zebu, while next to him an uninspired angel is putting black and white stripes on a rejected drawing of a horse he found in the wastepaper basket and is calling it the Zebra. The angel who is drawing Zebra went as far as to steal the first three letters of his animal's name from his silly pal who is drawing the ridiculous Zebu! Just like any classroom.

Those are some of the ideas, such as they are, which went into *Lion*. I mention them because I have a feeling that when I'm asked "How did you ever think of such a crazy idea?" the person who asked the question felt that the book was thought of in a moment, illustrated in a week, and printed in a day. There is a widespread feeling that doing children's books is a divertisement or hobby, never a full time job, and that it's quick and easy. I don't want to discourage people who want to dash off a children's book, but I would like to slow them down a bit. Thank you.

The Golden Age

By HARRY BEHN

WHENEVER I meet children's librarians, or people who write and illustrate, or select and publish, or review children's books, I wonder if children, as a general category, amaze you as much as they do me. My own three when they were small, my two granddaughters who still are, children in Connecticut, California, Italy, England, Indian children in Arizona or Mexico, all have so many customs in common that I think of childhood as a sort of separate nation without boundaries. This suggests, I suppose, that our adult divisions are acquired and unnatural, often exciting, but at times a bit troublesome. The differences between adult societies are so great that I wonder we get along together as well as we do. Sometimes it seems as if the only ambassadors all nations hold in common respect are under five.

Perhaps the mysterious rapport of children over the whole earth is the result of their simply not knowing any better than to be themselves. Compared to us, they are certainly honest; and wise in a way, for there is wisdom in being one's own self and yet able to deal with paradox. Children are perfectly at ease with opposites. An adult is inclined to deny a fact that does not fit some pattern he has assembled, in art, politics, ethics, or simply manners. But a child sees nothing strange in being at once a total individualist and a conservative citizen of traditional childhood; in being nobody in the world but himself, and yet everybody and everything seen, imagined, tasted, touched, smelled, bumped into, listened to, or swallowed whole, intentionally or by accident. Such singleness in multiplicity is astounding, and to me more admirable than our grownup impersonations clinging to us like pitch to the tar-baby. Always at the heart of a normal child is himself.

I am a partisan of childhood, because of its paradoxical, protean pliancy and its integrity, which makes me critical at times of certain "mature" propensities. I don't think we are more self-centered than children, but simply more rigid, sometimes without having either a self or a center. Too much of our living is done out there somewhere, looking for some undefined, intangible something such as authority, or importance, or power. I am often puzzled why people who have responsibilities so often play trivial games with serious matters and are so serious about things of no importance — of no importance to me, I mean.

There, you see, I have proved myself to be a characteristic adult, judging with my own evaluation and incomplete evidence. Each of us measures his own fantasy with an elastic yardstick, stepping all over others to project it into the world. What an intricate web we have woven! Some of our designs are magnificent, but some sag like old cobwebs full of dust, and some are stretched out so taut I wonder they don't snap in our faces.

Only a few years ago, civilization was more like a tropical sea, flowing with indolent wars over the benighted, bringing trade and tyranny, sanitation and disease, but always enlightenment, and, as drums rattled and trumpets blew, flowing on over more backward but still placid villages.

No longer does progress so genially advance. As the world shrinks, speed has tossed into our faces new equations too involved even for electronic computation. Our tidal, floral, forested earth, spotted with a few cities, has become a seed of such minuscule proportion that the faintest breeze might blow it away. Under some cosmic microscope, what do we see? Brittle, brilliant crystals of thought flashing up instantly into things, wings, instruments, with purposes but no purpose; exuberant new flushes of health, and explosions of babies; phalanxes of money marching forth to conquer armies of panda bears seven feet tall made of synthetic plush; chrome-gleaming deactivated weapons to hang on Christmas trees; contraptions beeping in the black emptiness among the stars.

And here we are among our commodities, reading grown-up books reiterating the well-known mechanics of propagation, or relaxing our souls before images of cowboy mayhem!

Do children play such games? Of course, beep-beeping their space-guns, marching along in any of our shoddy parades, refusing to sleep at night without their football helmets strapped on their heads. How do we dare to laugh! At least *they* know when a game is a game. As the tune of life changes, they can instantly drop *their* simulations. We are not so limber, being committed to this or that "principle," being members of this or that mass, believing what we have become habituated to think we think.

This is no charge leveled at some bad persons out there in the world. I am as deeply involved as anyone. But it does no harm, I think, to hold up one mysteriously simple culture beside an equally mysterious complex one. We might learn something.

Children are natural critics of complexity. With one glance at our contrived world, bought and sold for beans less fertile than Jack's, they are apt to turn from our merchandise to play happily with a few pebbles that are houses and a twig that is a tree.

Obviously, civilization must be simplified and made more honest. We must discover how to live together in moderate amity. It will take a good deal of imagination to bring so many opposites into harmony, to create an inwardly desired cohesive order out of so many contradictory compulsions, to design a civilization permitting all decent variables to live together in at least a semblance of freedom and understanding.

Perhaps only because they are fresh to experience, children are insatiably curious, wanting to understand everything. Our "mature" curiosity too seldom ranges beyond the areas in which we earn our living and relax from our labors. We are not notably addicted to a passionate desire for understanding. If only we might add our treasure of all recorded knowledge to the child's fresh eagerness to understand, then our social, economic, and political disorder might begin to assume reasonable clarity.

I suppose it is unscientific to suggest that children are born with an instinctive citizenship in their own friendly nation of childhood, with inherited rituals and traditions. But how is it that they understand each other so easily, that all over the world they play the same games, counting each other in or out with almost the same gibberish, dreaming the same dreams? How do they communicate these formalities? Who teaches them the same rules for winning a game fairly? How do they know, as I know they know, that a dream is a dream, and a puppy is a puppy?

If only we grownups could make such distinctions between fantasy and reality, between facts and the truth! But how passionately we insist that God is commensurable. and therefore isn't, or is infinite and is! That only mankind matters, or the individual. How often we dream up a good thing and put it to work as an engine of demolition!

Still, out of our considerable shame, I do believe a better world is emerging. How could it be otherwise? There are more — by the millions more — gentle people who want a better world for their children — a world not only more secure (since we are learning how lifeless security alone may be), but better. Everywhere school bells are ringing; everywhere there is a deep hunger for purpose and meaning; and love, everywhere, love for children; and hope.

There is no way now for us to give up our ICBMs, isotopes, automation, antibiotics, aircraft, automobiles, or plumbing. None of us wants to, although we know that each promises a spawn of problems as yet only dimly foreseen, some of which even now smother us with anxieties. We must go on with our things, on through increasing complexity toward a possible simplicity, a possible freedom. But we must discover anew that in spite of our rush toward outer space, there is still an inner space, free and timeless. Especially is this the dominion of childhood, that world-wide nation without boundaries or wars.

A long time ago it was said that unless ye become as little children ye shall not enter into the kingdom of heaven. In matters of fact and information, children are blissfully ignorant, so *that* is not what is meant. How then must we become? I would say, we must be more respectful of mystery, more aware of beauty and wonder. Of course, children are fed and clothed without effort of their own and have more time for wonder. Also, they are loved.

There is another attitude which I remember from my own childhood, and have further confirmed in my children when they were small and more recently in my grandchildren. It is a way of looking at time. To a child, time is simply eternity. Time does not take away; it gives, adds to, makes everything grow, naturally. Nothing changes into something it isn't. Everything becomes only more itself. Nothing dies.

Geared to speed as we are, we are justly afraid of time, especially if we see nothing before us but extinction. A child *knows* he has another life before him — ours. And a wonderful life it seems.

What I have described is simply faith. In faith there is no fear, at least no panic. So let us learn from children the courage of faith. And the bravest thing we can do in this world is to be kind. So let us be kind — at first as a practical measure. We might get used to it.

Out of a belief in the thoughts I have expressed, ten years ago I began my present business of writing for children. Now I can see how it actually started when I was four years old, when my older sister read me a story I detested, *Sanford and Merton,* a prodigiously moral narrative about a very clean and revoltingly good little boy, who inspired me to want to be as dirty and bad as I could be, forever. I made a pretty good start by giving my sister's dolls a bath in a barrel of roofing tar. After I was properly spanked, and forgiven, I crawled off into a corner and thought my first conscious thought, which was that some day I would make a book about a muddy little boy who liked to be muddy!

Soon after this incident, the course of my future altered slightly when I decided to be a poet — an absurd ambition as everyone knows, except children, or Indians who have totems compelling them to make songs whether they want to or not. I was unaware of it at the time, but I also had a totem. Indian totems are usually lizards or owls or some such creatures. Mine, however, was — I should say, is — a sort of truant officer concerned with the whole fabric of my life, a tag end of which is still in the future. Almost the whole of it was in the future when this guardian angel of mine began his meddling. Since he resembled, both in character and appearance, a P. G. Wodehouse butler, with wings, his name is, appropriately, Giles. Polite but firm, pleasant, knowing his place, Giles is nothing if not determined. It was his idea to make a poet of me. This is how it happened.

In 1903, on my first day in kindergarten, there he was, fussing over me, confusing me as I skipped round the mulberry bush, playing little tunes on his harp as London Bridge came crashing down. I wanted to go home, and so he offered me, not an apple, but a jar of delicious library paste, which I proceeded to eat; for which crime I was exiled to the cloak room. This was also a storage room, with a big sunny window and a window seat and shelves full of stacks of colored paper and boxes of colored chalk, and cubes and pyramids and tetrahedrons all brightly colored, and a few books. Inside this delightful prison (which had a good echo) I howled, until Miss Westervelt tripped in trembling and tried to quiet me. Hoping to read me into at least a snuffle, she reached for a book. That book might well have been another copy of you-know-what. Happily it wasn't. Because Giles (I am sure of it) handed down to Miss Westervelt a copy of William Blake's *Songs of Innocence,* conveniently opened to a poem which said, directly to me, as I nursed the last precious hiccup of my anguish:

> Piping down the valleys wild,
>   Piping songs of pleasant glee,
> On a cloud I saw a child,
>   And he laughing said to me:
>
> "Pipe a song about a lamb!"
>   So I piped with merry cheer.
> "Piper, pipe that song again";
>   So I piped: he wept to hear.
>
> "Drop thy pipe, thy happy pipe;
>   Sing thy songs of happy cheer."
> So I sang the same again,
>   While he wept with joy to hear.
>
> "Piper, sit thee down and write
>   In a book, that all my read."
> So he vanish'd from my sight,
>   And I pluck'd a hollow reed,

On Making a Book for a Child

By Taro Yashima

AS I have never made any academic study of children and never even read an article written about children, I cannot possibly consider myself as a specialist about children. My feeling is very confidenceless.

Anyhow, I begin. I was born and grew up in a southern village in Japan, and from the time I was a little boy I was very fond of the children younger than myself.

Even in the period of my early youth when I was suspicious and nihilistic toward everything and everybody, with no faith in the world at all, I could not be negative in my feeling toward the children. In that one gift — to feel the unique beauty, the innocent and helpless beauty of children — I think I was a little unusual.

Years later I was asked to put all my knowledge and capability into teaching an art class of children in a mission school. I did not know how to begin.

My son had begun to use a pencil when he was about a year and a half old, and he became far more eloquent in his watercolors than his speaking when he was four years old. It seemed that other children must have the same talent for expression, and somehow we managed, as each day brought more experience.

One day a mother came to the class with a little three-year-old boy. He carried a large shopping bag in which was a clean sheet of paper and a crayon. He came stepping inch-by-inch, very frightened, and it was obvious that he did not know what drawing is. He sat for a long time without doing anything at all, even after I had asked him, "Can you make a triangle?" and he had answered, "Yes."

Finally he made a tiny tiny triangle way down in the corner of his paper. His classmates teased him saying, "It looks like the head of an ant."

"Yes, it is the head of an ant," he said, and put body and legs to it. Then he made a house from a larger triangle and it grew into a trolley car, and then he made more ants — hundreds of ants and more houses and streets — until he had created a "City scene of ants" such as no one could possibly have imagined.

In some such way as this the thirty children in my art class were able to do splendid drawings which even their parents could not believe.

This was the period of the Japanese invasion of China, and more and more men around us were being drafted and returned dead. I myself was think-

[47]

ing of death and also waiting for a draft-paper every day. I did not want to die and found out that it was because I was positively attached to the people.

At the same time I could not take up my paint brushes any more, as I was realizing that the meaning of all the canvases I had done was unbearably shallow.

One day I was on a trolley car. I saw a middle-aged man with his son, about the age of my five-year-old. I could be sure that the man also was expecting a draft-paper any day, and was trying not to waste a moment with his son. I could see it in the way he held the boy on his lap and he covered his son's knees with both his hands. I never had felt the meaning of the human body so deeply and of course I never had made it reflect in my canvas. I thought that to present such meanings I would have to make a new study from the very beginning and I wanted to study the Western masters to see how they had painted what they understood.

I am sure this decision in such a difficult period was also due largely to the inspiration that came from the fresh vision and imagination of the children in my art class.

And so we came to this country. Our life here was completely separated from children as we left our son on the other side. It was ten years later and two years after the end of World War II before our son, now fifteen, could join us. At about the same time our daughter was born.

And then for almost four years I was beaten flat by an ulcer. But, being flat, I had plenty of time to think and it was inevitable that I should check over my life's experiences and re-form myself and my art from the very beginning.

And, very fortunately and unexpectedly, this struggle was helped by the fact that I was able to live with our new-born daughter so intimately. I was able not only to observe every moment of our daughter's growth but also to root out a certain prejudice toward women that had existed in me more or less as a result of my upbringing in Japan. Our daughter, who was two years old or so, used to put her cheek on mine whenever I had an ulcer pain. If it were not for my illness I never would have known that such a gentle human being could exist in such a little helpless baby.

I wanted to thank this little life and tell some nice stories to make this little girl happy.

Although I had stories which were told by my grandmother and father and read by myself, somehow they all seemed lifeless to express my feeling. So then I thought that perhaps if I could recall the joyful experiences of my childhood and tell them to her just as they happened they might recreate the same joy in her.

The Village Tree was a tree which stood deep in my memory as a symbol of my childhood. I had no idea of publishing that *Village Tree*. I just asked myself — why that tree stands so patiently in my memory; why that tree could be a symbol of my childhood. Why so?

Starting from such questions, I got closer to that tree and looked up from this side and that side. I climbed up on every branch and swam around under the tree to find out the reasons which made the joy in the memories. As I stated before, I did it for our daughter.

Plenty to Watch was done in the same way. It takes a long time to make a book for a child.

Often before I had wanted to publish picture books for children. The reason I was not able to realize my wish is that I went about it the wrong way. Finding the right way has taken half a lifetime. But still I have found it and I know that the impressions we have been getting from the outside world are astonishingly richer in us than we realize until we recall them for a child who is dear to us.

Well, as I mentioned in the beginning, I am not a specialist about children. But, as a human being, I cannot help imagining that children will grow and face many sorts of struggle that may even bring them to despair at times. I cannot help hoping that children will live through all their difficulties and I cannot help having the desire to give them something to help them through — these children who are innocent, helpless, and beautiful and ready to grow with such splendid possibilities.

The world is wide. Everything in it can be used to make books for children. But I think the theme of these should be, "This earth is beautiful! Living is wonderful! Believe in humankind!"

A Storyteller's Approach to Children's Books

By RUTH SAWYER

I AM speaking tonight on storytelling as an approach to children's books and reading. But first I would have you believe with me that storytelling is an art unto itself. It is a traditional art, a folk art, creating from the past and the present those experiences which we know must enrich the lives of all children. During the time the story is told those experiences live, carried on the spoken word, strengthened by the storyteller's art of recreating. She draws her listeners into the happenings of the story, making them an integral part of it. They share in those vivid emotions called forth: expectancy, wonder, courage, compassion, curiosity, and delight in the fun and the absurdities.

This intimacy in sharing makes of a story told a far more memorable experience than a story read by a child to himself; in this lies one of the indisputable values of storytelling. In other words, did storytellers do no more than recreate that vast, imperishable heritage of folk and fairy tales, hero tales, legends, and myths — along with the finest of the modern stories, I think we all must grant that storytelling has proved indelibly its place in the growing, developing, and reaching-out years of childhood.

Having established this let us go on to a further value of storytelling; its use in relation to books and reading.

We have two well marked problems in both libraries and schools today. The first is to keep our readers abreast of the welter of new books being published each year. Publishers' lists have doubled and trebled in length since the 1930s. And the second problem is the urgent need to keep the fine old books read and cherished. Large library systems are able to have on their staffs special readers to evaluate the new books, select the best for library use. But what of the schools? Teachers say frankly they can no longer keep up with the new books and writers. And what of the hundreds of small libraries and school libraries? Here there is apt to be too much random choosing, and so often the best books slip by unnoticed. And what of bewildered parents? I think we all know how deep disappointment can go with that boy or girl who gets the wrong book given to him — or even taken out on a library card.

Here, I think, is where storytelling can be of great help. Always one, sometimes two new books can have five-minute tellings during a storyhour — enough told to whet interest, invite expectancy, and send listeners back to the library with a definite idea whether this is the book they want to read. So much enthusiastic reading can follow on the heels of such a story! How many times I have heard shouted across the library or school yard: "Hi there! I've got a good book."

Ellis Credle's *Tall Tales From the High Hills* offered a fine Halloween story, "The Voice in the Jug." For months after the telling there was no copy idle on the shelves. For older boys and girls I found a rich harvest of reading reaped from a five-minute telling of James Ramsey Ullman's *Banner in the Sky*. Potential rock climbers read it avidly; classes studying Switzerland found a good deal more than geography and social study in the book's challenge. Seventh and eighth graders could measure to their own years and courage Rudi Matt's patience and strength.

To drop down to first graders — where our readers begin — I found that never-failing delight in Palmer Bown's little book about *Cheerful* — "a story of a mouse, maybe two mice, or four mice." It is not easy to find something happy to tell about Easter. But here was stuff guaranteed to keep wriggles out of a roomful of first graders; and afterwards the teachers of second and third grade got copies to read to their children.

These are but fragmentary illustrations of how new books may be sent forth to find those readers eager for them. I know of no greater delight than to watch faces during the short telling and realise how a wise selecting of books with a wide angle of appeal will be caught on the instant by those individual minds alerted to them.

It is even so with the old books that are in danger of being overlooked. In many libraries I have found Washington Irving and Nathaniel Hawthorne completely lost. Louisa May Alcott's *Little Women* is read — but what of her *Jo's Boys* and *Under the Lilacs* and a host of others? Except for *Treasure Island* Stevenson is rarely read. The *Just So Stories* find frequent readers; but Kipling's *Jungle Books* need to be brought into one storyhour after another that they may not be forgotten. I have found boys and girls listening with the same expectation and zest as they listened a generation ago as Mowgli creeps into the wolf's cave. They held the same tense eagerness for Father and Mother Wolf's decision: would they give Mowgli up to the lame tiger or protect him? And defend him later on the council rock? Dull indeed those ears of childhood that have never heard that ringing command from Akela — the lone wolf: "Look well, oh wolves, look well!" Here our boys and girls take part in the fine drama of adventure; and they experience it again in the story of "Rikki-Tikki-Tavi" and in "Toomai of the Elephants." And who of us would not keep ripe in the minds of our teen agers, especially in the minds of the boys, that fine sea yarn: *Captains Courageous*?

Lawrence Housman's *Doorway into Fairyland* and *Moonshine and Clover* are no longer on the shelves of many libraries; and yet I have found his *Chinese Fairytale* hold spellbound the boys and girls of Junior High. The children today all have read and loved Eleanor Farjeon's *Silver Curlew*; but the "Martin Pippin" books are forgotten. And yet think of how much fun would be lost if no storyteller ever told again *Tom Cobble* or *Elsie Piddock*! And what of Charles Dickens's *Magic Fishbone* and the amazingly wise Princess Alicia; what of John Ruskin's *King of the Golden River* and Charles Kingsley's *Water Babies*? What of the books of George MacDonald and our own Howard Pyle! Here are only a few of that glorious host of old books, waiting to be brought from the shelves and have the breath of life blown into them by all the storytellers around the world. They make a goodly company — vital and universal in their appeal. Let us keep them a part of childhood's living heritage.

The Greek and Norse hero tales come heavily scored for constant telling. As a listener I stand aside from myself as a storyteller, and I am spellbound to watch what can happen with a group of middle-age children when the story of *The Chimera* is told. I like the gentle beginning Hawthorne gives the story — with the gathering of the farmer, the old man, the maiden, and the boy at the Fountain of Pirene. When the stranger joins them, the enchanted bridle in his hand, and asks about the winged horse and all but the boy deny his existence — then does expectation soar. And from the moment the boy calls across to the stranger — "I have seen the winged horse" — the story mounts on wings of its own to the ending, wholly wonderfull, wholly satisfying.

The stories of King Midas, Perseus, Jason, Hercules all offer fine invitations to a reading of the Greek tales; but I have found the story of Bellerephon, Pegasus, and the slaying of the Chimera by far the best to start with. It may strike many as odd that I have followed these hero tales of a time long ago and of countries far away with modern hero tales and found they made a good rounding out for young imaginations. Lou Gehrig, Babe Ruth, Abraham Lincoln, and Albert Schweitzer mould their lives in different forms of courage — of self-sacrifice, spiritual strength, and a final conquering — but all have in common the same dedication to service.

From the many folk tales collected by Jeremiah Curtin nearly a century ago there is one I particulary like to use:

> The King of Ireland's Son set forth on the early road and met up with a wise woman of the lough. To him she said: "Dear lad, that you are, stop at the first market town. There in stall or peddler's pack you will be

choosing the right thing to take with you on your quest. If the choosing be right — you will go the lee, long way with a lilt in your heart, the wind at your back — and you, journeying in the hollow of God's hand."

This is a free rendering from the Gaelic. Whenever the tale has been told it has made a deep marking on the faces of listeners. I think not a boy or girl but has sat tense with hard wishing that the King of Ireland's Son may make the right choice. Herein lies a universal appeal and truth; and it is because of this universalness in folk tales that I feel we should keep on telling them as long as there are tongues to tell and young ears to listen. Childhood has its own trust in life and the world, and the greatest part of folk literature vindicates this trust of childhood. It is altogether right that, of the three brothers starting on adventure, it should be the youngest, the one looked down upon by his older clever brothers, who succeeds. For it is the youngest, the simpleton, who stops along the road to free the bird from its snare, to help the old woman with her bundle of fagots, or to share his meal with some poor fellow or creature. Compassion and generosity are good traveling companions. And when the quest is over and the hero finds that his brothers, or the other fellows, have not returned, he goes back to free them from enchantment or death. And that is right. It adds decency and humility to the meaning of the tale.

And so collections of Grimm, Andersen, Jacobs, Lang, Perrault, Ella Young, Padraic Colum, James Stephens, and W. B. Yeats should be kept in circulation. These old tales belong to Childhood Past, Childhood Present, and Childhood to Come. We know their appeal is eternally young and lasting.

There are three books that are neither old nor recent but which I have told constantly during the past year. May I recall them?

The first is James Dougherty's *Daniel Boone*. Because of its format — fine as it is — it has been overlooked too often. The boys and girls of the upper elementary grades are apt to class it as "another picture book" and so pass it by. It has been exciting to bring this book to a storyhour for fifth and sixth graders and watch what happens. There is always a sudden awakening to the grandeur and challenge of our pioneer days — a growing realization of the vastness of that wilderness that now makes up our five Appalachian states. I begin with what the author says of Boone:

> You were a free, singing rider in a lost dream.
> Your name still echoes in the mountain passes, it is a whisper and a heartbeat along the old trail.

Then on to where James Dougherty lets Boone speak for himself: he speaks to the youth of America, the youth of today:

> "Rise up you lanky sons of democracy, of Tennessee, Texas, Vermont and New Hampshire, of Missouri, Ohio, Oregon, and the rest of the glorious brotherhood of states.
>
> Pray to the God of your fathers that their spirit be upon you — that you have the enduring courage to cut a straight path through the wilderness against oppression for generations marching on to higher freedoms. . . .
>
> Riding towards the sun, singing in the cornbrakes, singing in the tough spots, chanting: Democracy, here we come! Shouting to the bullies, the tyrannies, the hosts of darkness, shouting with the seven times mighty shout of Jerico 'No surrender!' "

Great words! And I find our children today like the swing and beauty of our rich English tongue when they have a chance to hear it spoken with pride and simplicity.

Daniel Boone's makes a crackling good story; and our youth, stifled under the welter of present day civilization, need this free, breathing record of pioneer times.

My second book is *Amos Fortune, Free Man* by Elizabeth Yates. Here is a book we cannot afford to forget — not from Arkansas to Harlem.

I begin by giving the epitaph in the little cemetery at Jaffry, New Hampshire:

> Sacred to the memory of Amos Fortune.
> Who was born free in Africa,
> a slave in America.
> He purchased his liberty,
> Professed Christianity,
> Lived reputably,
> Died hopefully.

This may seem to many a strange way to begin an invitation to reading; but I have found it grips the interest at once. Then I go back to the beginning of the book, to equatorial Africa and the season for planting the corn. Here the telling can be kept brief, a vivid picture of the young prince Atmun and his tribe, the Atmunshi.

Here Elizabeth Yates gives a sharp-drawn backdrop for the rest of the story, in words that are strong and sure:

> Night came down swiftly over the forest; after the snuffing out of the sun, darkness, the bright appearing stars. No silence came with the darkness for this was a night alive with song and movement. . . . Time for planting when the earth was about to be reborn.

The great drum sets the rhythm, small drums follow, voices chant:

> Earth, our Mother, Sun, our Father,
> Watch while we plant.
> Moon, our Sister, Rain, our Brother,
> Aid the seeds to bear fruit....

And then it was that the slavers came and put chains on the young prince who became Amos Fortune. With rare dignity, good humor, and persistence he made his way among strangers, learned their language, learned the complexities of a civilized life. He became a tanner of repute; to stand at last among his white brothers a free man. Loved and honored for his humility, his generosity, and his integrity. Truly, here is the stuff from which comes a true hero tale.

And what of my third story? It is one to tell at this spring season. Unfortunately few young people are apt to discover this book for themselves. But when it is discovered for them, how completely do they enter into the wonder and absurdities of this world of small creatures. How completely do they become a part of their loyalties and the beauty and miracle that lie along the river bank, or lie hidden in the deep woods! Here one begins at the beginning; and, except for a slight cutting, tells the tale exactly, in Kenneth Graham's own words:

> Mole had been working hard all morning, spring-cleaning his little house. Brooms and dusters, ladders and steps, pails and whitewash....
> But spring was moving in the air above and in the earth below. Was it a wonder that he threw down his brush and said: "Bother!" and "Oh Blow!" and "Hang spring-cleaning!"
> So he made for his little tunnel and scraped and scratched and scratched and scrooged, muttering, "Up we go!" until at last his snout came into the sunlight and he found himself rolling in the long grass....
> He crossed the meadow and an elderly rabbit called out — "Hold up! Sixpence for passing!"
> "Onion sauce" said the mole, and went on.... It all seemed too good to be true....
> Suddenly he stood by the river. Never had he seen a river. It was all ashake, all aquiver, all chatter and bubbles.... Mole trotted along beside it, bewitched, spellbound. Then he looked across. There was a hole in the bank and his eye caught a small brown face with whiskers. It was Water Rat.
> "Hullo, Mole!"
> "Hullo, Rat"
> "Like to come over?"... And then Rat unfastened a rope and slipped into a little boat. Mole's whole heart went out to it. Rat sculled across, held out a forepaw; and to his great rapture Mole found himself in the stern of a real boat. "It's been a wonderful day", said Mole.

"Never been in a boat before"....

"What!" said Rat.... Believe me there's nothing like messing about in
boats."

One need tell no further. Mole and Rat and Badger and Toad are back again
in the heart and imagination of childhood. *The Wind in the Willows* is off
the shelves for a spring-time of reading.

Here then is an approach to old books, too often forgotten, or to new
books, not yet discovered, that can be made during any storyhour. We have
found it to bring a goodly response among regular readers. But what of the
slow or the lazy reader? The printed page, long paragraphs, narrow margins,
and lack of imagination, all seem to lay a roadblock between these readers
and high adventure in books. Unless we catch these slow and lazy ones
before they reach their teens they are never likely to know much of books
and the rare delight and good fellowship to be found in them.

Difficult appetites, whether they be for reading or for food, can be coaxed.
I know of no more compelling way to do this than by a storyhour. Here good
readers and non-readers experience together that invitation that all good
tales offer and that assurance that is carried by the spoken word — that
here is something that will warrant further interest. This sharing of enjoyment is contageous; and so often the good reader will steer the non-reader
to the book and say, "Better take it out. It's a jolly good book. I've read it
twice."

And what of imaginations, or lack of imaginations? Just what can our
imaginations do for us? Do they not invest us with that power of the mind
to touch those people, places, events, not present, and make them become
living things, actual experiences? Does not imagination become for each of
us our own particular fairy wand that can transform whatever it reaches
into reality for the moment? Let us not forget how much storytellers touch
and transform with their art. And is there anything more certain than that
during the span of a tale dull imaginations may be kindled by the response
of these listeners wholly aware of the enchantment and all that a fairytale
can compass? I can think of few greater tragedies in childhood than to have
a boy or girl grow into adulthood with withered imagination. Years of living
with never a fairy wand within reach! May I quote Edna St Vincent Millay's
"The Unexplorers"?

> There was a road ran past our house,
>   Too lovely to explore.
> I asked my mother once, she said

That if you followed where it led
It brought you to the milkman's door.
That's why I have not traveled more.

Charles Morgan who has so much that is wise to say about childhood, and
his own boyhood in particular, would have those of us concerned with any
of the needs and activities of childhood remember that the growing mind
works two ways: from within out, and from without in. He well remembers
how he stood in everlasting judgment and evaluation as he looked out upon
the world of people and events outside himself. And then how, standing in
this world, he looked within, in judgment on himself. He so rightly points
out that it is here the growing child becomes conscious of his separateness,
out of which can come that terrible sense of aloneness that may grip an adult
for the rest of his life.

Charles Morgan tells of standing often before his own shelf of books, uncertain whether to take a book out for fear that if he read it again he might
lose that keen enjoyment, that sense of being a part of it all, sharing its adventure and its challenge. In other words, he was fearful that any book
might betray him as some people had.

It is here that I think those of us who work with books for young people
must be gravely concerned. We must keep in mind the great need of estab-
lishing that sense of universal belonging that every child must grow with, as
well as to vindicate their trust in his two worlds. We must remember there
is a wide area of sensitivity in more young minds than we dream of. Everywhere about us stands the young potential of the artist, the leader, the
statesman, the builder, the musician.

May I recall to you something of Robert Browning's poem: "Death in the
Desert"? I use it constantly — for it is something I need to remember myself — in all that I do. Take it as a symbol of much that I have been trying
to say to you tonight.

The poem is concerned with the death of John of Patmos. Like many a
dying man he looks back on life, testing it, and in some places giving it a
fresh revelation. He speaks of man having not one soul but three souls. First
the soul that *does*, with feet firmly planted on the earth. Second, the soul
that *knows*, mounted on the shoulders of the first soul. Finally the soul that
is, mounted on the shoulders of the first and second souls. It is this soul that
is eternally reaching for the stars.

For those of us whose service lies with young people, with books and the
telling of stories, I take it to be an easy and a frequent matter to serve the
needs of the soul that does and the soul that knows. These souls are partic-

ularly in evidence with those everyday children we contact. "I want a book about baseball." "I want a book about building radios." "I want a book about Japan — or Indonesia — or Mexico."

But what of the boy who is reaching for faith, for inspiration, for that constant affirmation that he is not different, that he is not lost or alone! We never know, I think, from what we can read as childhood runs so swiftly by us, how many there may be reaching for the stars. But let us never forget they are there — and let us reach with them.

Poetry and Children: "This Way, Delight!"

By Amelia H. Munson

T HE SEASONED lecturer, I have often observed, invariably opens his discourse by expressing his thanks for the honor done him and his extreme pleasure at the prospect before him, then by lamenting his own ineptitude, and finally by inveighing — in the most polite terms — against the wording of his topic (which, presumably, he had agreed to weeks before). It is either so broad a theme that he can only touch upon its varied aspects in the pitifully brief time at his disposal, or it is so difficult to define that he fears he will become a trespasser if he moves in any direction, or it is too specialized for him (who is clearly no expert) to add anything of value to the already established corpus.

This is not the way he talked to himself in his own room as he was attempting to prepare some remarks. He was pecking petulantly at his topic. "What am I to do with this?" he mutters. "What am I supposed to say about it?" And Conscience smartly retorts, "Something new and brilliant and profound."

I should like to adhere to this tradition by thanking those who were so generous as to give me this opportunity, for I hold in high esteem and affection the founder of The New York Public Library's Work with Children, the significance of which — and its continuity — are marked by this series of annual lectures. And I count it an honor to be associated with the three gracious and gifted speakers who have already appeared in the series (any one of whom, by the way, could easily have dealt with tonight's topic along with her own). I shall however pass quickly over the "lament" or apology. Since inadequacies will shortly become all too apparent, it ill behooves me to call attention to them in advance. As for the topic, here let me linger. It is amazing how the appeal or the challenge a topic presents at the time of its acceptance — that gloriously free and far-off time — alters or fades or assumes a formidable appearance in direct proportion to the approach of the inexorable hour. The enchantment of distance falls away, and a sombre pall of grayness — partly fog, partly funk — envelops it.

For what can I say to you, who are so at home in this field, that shall be new? And yet how can anyone deal truly with this dual subject and fail to be new, as the day is new, "new every morning and fresh every evening"? That is childhood, the dew and sunshine still upon it, each child a new creation unlike any other, showing unexpected facets as we seek to observe without disturbing. We are always fascinated by what we perceive and by what forever eludes us. And this is poetry, too. Poetry and children are akin in many ways. Both may be studied on various levels, or may be thoroughly enjoyed without study or even understanding. Both delude us into thinking we are thinking, whereas, instead, they "tease us out of thought," for the springs that are touched upon are far deeper than those of the mind and reach into our store of ancient and racial knowledge. Both look out upon the universe with new eyes and find all strange and wonderful, mysterious and yet congruous and acceptable. Both contain far more than their immediate creators have put into them, and these qualities emerge as our capacity for understanding increases. Both are paradoxical combinations of eager communication and baffling reticence, and it is left to us to "make straight in the desert a highway" of communion between us.

What can I bring you that is new? I bring you DELIGHT, as promised in the title. And that title, "This Way, Delight!", was lifted from Herbert Read's beautiful anthology of poems for the young (of any age), and Sir Herbert lifted it from a line of old John Fletcher, and what we need at this moment is a street crier to sing his "Song in the Wood":

> This way, this way, come and hear
> You that hold these pleasures dear;
> Fill your ears with our sweet sound,
> Whilst we melt the frozen ground.
>
> This way, come, make haste, O fair!
> Let your clear eyes gild the air;
> Come, and bless us with your sight;
> This way, this way, seek delight!

If delight is not to be found in childhood and in poetry, I know not where to search it out. And if it is not a new experience, "something new and strange," in these —— days (better left uncharacterized), I leave it to you to name a greater rarity. We spend our days brooding over a clutch of worries and suspicions and hatch out fears, monstrous, paralyzing fears, to which we feel bound to give all our attention. I could say, "The valiant never taste of Death but once," and you will supply the preceding line. "This is the trouble with us all," cries the poet,

> This is the trouble with us all
> That we see under the shell, and we see under the inner shell,
> And we see under what lies under what lies under . . .
> Grant that some shadow of awe, some gold fog of marvel
> Cover for once this terrible sun of our eyes.

And yet another poet mocks us fretful souls:

> There is no time
> No time
> There is no time
> Not even for a kiss
> Not even for this
> Not even for this rhyme
>
> It is May
> And blossoms sway
> In lifted snow
> Under the moon
> I only know
> That I cannot stay
> For today is May
> And tomorrow June
>
> An arrow shot
> From an idiot's bow
> That is my lot
> And I must go
>
> There is no time
> No time
> There is no time
> Not even for a kiss
> Not even for this
> Not even for this rhyme
> No!

But today is not May nor is tomorrow June. Today is April, harbinger of Spring, and I bid you look and listen:

> The sun was warm but the wind was chill.
> You know how it is with an April day
> When the sun is out and the wind is still,
> You're one month on in the middle of May.
> But if you so much as dare to speak,
> A cloud comes over the sunlit arch,
> A wind blows off a frozen peak,
> And you're two months back in the middle of March.

That was Sunday. This was yesterday

> The Spring that comes before the Spring
> And waits while boughs are thin and bare,
> A deepened light, a quickening,
> Annunciation in the air,
> Delight me more, though cold and brief,
> Than buds abounding, and the leaf.

And this is today:

> Nature's first green is gold,
> Her hardest hue to hold
> Her early leaf's a flower,
> But only so an hour.
>
> Then leaf subsides to leaf.
> So Eden sank to grief,
> So dawn goes down to day.
> Nothing gold can stay.

And *watch* for this:

> Loveliest of trees, the cherry now
> Is hung with bloom along the bough,
> And stands about the woodland ride
> Wearing white for Eastertide.
>
> Now of my threescore years and ten,
> Twenty will not come again,
> And take from seventy springs a score,
> It only leaves me fifty more,
>
> And since to look at things in bloom
> Fifty springs are little room,
> About the woodland I will go
> To see the cherry hung with snow.

There speaks the practical man as well as the poet, the "I will arise and go" man. And I am sure that there is a spring in his step as well as in the air.

For this old earth is still lovely, even though there's such a scramble to get away from it. "Earth's the right place for love / I don't know where it's likely to go better." It isn't standing still, either; it's spinning around four times as fast as any of our man-made satellites. That's a dizzying thought, but it leaves us unperturbed. *This* is terra firma, and it's ours. Not so the world. May I remind you?

> A Toad that lived at Albury Heath
> Wanted to see the world.
> "It isn't that I dislike the heath—
> It's a perfectly charming heath, of course,
> All this heather and all this gorse,
> All this bracken to lie beneath
> With its feathery fronds to the sky uncurled—
> It's as charming a heath as ever was found,
> But it's flat—and the world, they say, is round.

Yes, fancy, it's round," he said, "they tell me.
And wouldn't I like to go and see!
But there, it's a long way down the road
For a fellow that walks as slow as a toad.
If I had a horse, I'd go," said he,
"If only I had a horse!
Who's got a horse," he cried, "to lend me?"
Well, nobody had, you see.

But horses came to the Heath one day,
Mettlesome steeds in brave array
With prancing legs and dancing eyes
And crimson saddles that fall and rise
As round the galloping squadron flies,
And tents and stalls and cocoanut shies,
And races and a band and cheering!
"Hark!" said the Toad, "What's this I'm hearing?
It must be the World arrived, by the sound.
Now I'll see if it's really round."

Off he crawled to the thick of things,
And the crowd make crawling somewhat tiring.
"Dear me!" he said, "I wish I'd wings!
If this is the World," said he, perspiring,
"It's inconveniently full of feet!"
When a sudden voice said, "Look! How sweet!
Mummy, a Toad! Let's give him a treat.
It's not very safe for him here on the ground,
So I'll put him up on the merry-go-round!"

And before the Toad could answer, the floor began to slide,
The horses started prancing, and the riders settled to ride,
And they all moved faster, and the band began to play,
And away round he went with them — away and away and away,
Hurray!

So the Toad rode the roundabout, round and round and round.
No one minded him; he sat without a sound.
He rather liked the movement, he rather liked the tune,
He just rode the roundabout all the afternoon.

When the time to pay came, what did he do?
"Tuppence a ride! Tuppence a ride! How many for you?"
Some had ridden for one ride, some had ridden for two —
"Seventy-nine," the Toad cried. The boy said "Cool!"
"But never you mind," the Toad replied, "Here's an I O U."

"And now," he said, "I'll go, thanks. I want to be home for tea.
Another for nothing? No, thanks. Not any more for me!"

Home, holding the grasses,
Crawling a crooked road,
Slowly there passes
A very unsteady Toad.

"Well, and what have you found, Dear?
And what have you seen and heard?
Is the World really round, Dear?"
"Round?" he said, "My word!
Round?" said he, "You should feel it spin!
Roundest place I ever was in!
Round?" he chuckled, "It's that.
But it's rather," he said with a knowing wink,
"It's rather a giddy place, I think.
Give me a drop of the dew to drink,
And give me the Heath! — it's flat!"

Flat it may be, but it's familiar, and therefore beloved. There, for childhood,
is one of the most reassuring facts. "Here I go up in my swing / Now I go
down." And it is one of poetry's most magical qualities that because of its
strong, natural rhythms, reenforced usually with the expectancy it can create
and satisfy with end rhymes, it slips unobtrusively into our consciousness
and is as if it had always been there. "Poetry," says Keats, "should surprise
by a fine excess and not by singularity. It should strike the reader as a wording
of his own highest thoughts and appear almost a rembrance." "An indwell-
ing," Forster has called it. And Frost has said that the greatest compliment
anyone can pay his verses is a nod of the head, an acceptance, a recognition.

The strength of those lines in A Roundabout Turn and the variety of
rhythms used delight us as much as they do children. We may always be
sure that in genuine poetry the lines will stand. They may bend and sway,
they may even waver, as the "very unsteady Toad" caused one to do, but
they will not break. They can bear more than their own weight; they can
transport us in both senses of the word, in complete safety. It is the built-in
rhythm that permits the stress and guards against the ravages of fatigue,
from the simple, "One, two / Buckle my shoe," to the tidal "Out of the cradle,
endlessly rocking" and the majestic "Where wast thou when I laid the foun-
dation of the earth?" . . . When the morning stars sang together and all the
sons of God shouted for joy?" Fortunate he whose childhood embraces these
experiences and whose ear early becomes accustomed to the flexibility and
the sheer magnificence of our English language!

The rainbow comes and goes,
And lovely is the Rose,
The Moon doth with delight

> Look round her when the heavens are bare,
>   Waters on a starry night
>   Are beautiful and fair;
>   The sunshine is a glorious birth;
>   And yet I know, where'er I go,
> That there hath passed away a glory from the earth.

There is our recurring theme, Delight, again — "The moon doth with delight / Look round her when the heavens are bare," and, although those lines may be warped by some of our sardonic sophisticates of today to a significance never suspected by Wordsworth, the majesty of the stanza cannot be impaired. Throughout this great ode runs the constant laudation of childhood —

> There was a time when meadow, grove, and stream,
> The earth, and every common sight
>   To me did seem
>   Apparelled in celestial light,
> The glory and the freshness of a dream —

and —

> Delight and liberty, the simple creed
> Of childhood, whether busy or at rest,
> With new-fledged hope still fluttering in his breast —

and, as the poet looked about him in dismay ("The world is too much with us!") and looked back with longing, he tried to reconcile himself to the "aging process" —

> And O, ye Fountains, Meadows, Hills, and Groves,
> Forbode not any severing of our loves!
> Yet in my heart of hearts I feel your might;
> I only have relinquished one delight
> To live beneath your more habitual sway.
> I love the Brooks which down their channels fret
> Even more than when I tripped lightly as they;
> The innocent brightness of a new-born Day
>   Is lovely yet.

I used to think it wonderful that an old man could make philosophy into such lyric exuberance, and I rejoiced in the consolation it must have afforded him. Now that I have had time to look into hitherto unapprehended minutiae, I am both maddened and delighted. Had you realized that Wordsworth wrote this Ode on the Intimations of Immortality at the ripe old age of 35? Yes, in the years between 33 and 36. If I needed any reassurance of his possession of imaginative powers — and there are times, you know — I have it now. Thirty-five indeed! Someday, if I can bear it, I must find out how old Allingham was when he recollected —

> Four ducks on a pond,
> A grass-bank beyond,
> A blue sky of Spring,
> White clouds on the wing;
> What a little thing
> To remember for years —
> To remember with tears!

And here is a modern poet making sure that there will be a recollection:

GASOLINE LETTER
(After a motor trip)

> Not men had built this road, not men had planted
> These orchards, cleared these fields; we felt, unseen,
> A Gargantuan hand unroll the ribbon
> Under us, enchanting the machine;
> A Hand removing time with our smooth motion,
> Enchanting us to forgive the cruel year.
> Such happiness is supernatural — name it,
> It crumbles, and is fear.
> We were half afraid, watching the yellow willows
> Beside their silver sons, the blue increase
> Of sky, leaving its clouds behind; the tawny
> Autumn touch in the ash-trees; the sunned fleece
> Of upland pastures; drinking the wind; meeting
> The lakes' dark gentle eyes.
>   And we were mute,
> Crying, Remember — thinking of famine, Remember
> The true taste of this fruit.

May I let my mind wander a moment, not from poetry, but to a poem associated with this in many ways?

> Once, on a cliff, I saw perfection happen.
> The full gold moon was balanced on the sea,
> Just as the red sun rested on the moor.
> The summer evening ripened and fell open;
> And people walking through that fruit's rich core
> Were suddenly what they were meant to be —
> Quiet and happy, softly-moving, lovely,
> With still, translucent faces and clear eyes,
> And all their heads and bodies brightly rimmed
> With delicate gold. So radiantly, so gravely,

> These people walked, so crowned, so golden-limbed,
> The cliff seemed like the edge of Paradise.

And if we go now from a New England cliff to London's Strand and back
to the days when Charles Lamb was a small "Bluecoat Boy" from Christ's
Hospital, you will find the connection:

> I met an angel in the Strand
> with an umbrella in his hand,
> talking with Paradisal joy
> to a bewildered Bluecoat boy.
> "And so," he said, "I understand
> this also is a Golden Strand
> that has, like Heaven, for example,
> an edifice they call the Temple,
> and leads by such another Bar
> as ours, to what they tell me would be witty
> to name The Uncelestial City.
> Well, well, let us examine it!"
> And while he spoke, the place was lit
> with some strange glory. Tired faces
> shone like the sun in country places,
> and people's voices sounded, when
> they spoke, like chords from Beethoven;
> the motor-buses had the hot
> splendour of a chariot;
> the houses by the Aldwych were
> as arrogant as Lucifer;
> the island-churches, like a crowd
> of golden starlings, cried aloud,
> till none could say which were the bells,
> and which were simply miracles;
> the very paving-stones were led,
> enchantingly astonishéd,
> into a crazy pattern, laid
> to trap the moss in ambuscade.
> Indeed the whole excited town
> glowed like a shy, delicious noun,
> when some great poet lets it live
> at last, beside its adjective.
>
> And then I saw, like a superb
> hawker, the angel at the curb
> set London working like a toy —
> and give it to the Bluecoat boy.

It takes a poet to make our great men walk the streets again, as Lamb walked
through London all his life (after the angel had set it working for him). It

took our own Robinson to give us our most vivid portrait of Shakespeare.
And since his birthday is now so near, perhaps we may be permitted a slight
sally. (Ben Jonson is speaking.)

You are a friend, then, as I make it out,
Of our man Shakespeare, who, alone of us,
Will put an ass's head in fairyland
As he would add a shilling to more shillings,
All most harmonious — and out of his
Miraculous, inviolable increase
Fills Ilion, Rome, or any town you like
Of ancient time with timeless Englishmen. . . .

He's all at odds with all the unities,
And what's yet worse it doesn't seem to matter;
He treads along through Time's old wilderness
As if the tramp of all the centuries
Had left no roads — and there are none for him. . . .

I'll meet him out alone of a bright Sunday,
Trim, rather spruce, and quite the gentleman,
"What, ho, my lord!" say I. He doesn't hear me;
Wherefore I have to pause and look at him.
He's not enormous, but one looks at him.
A little on the round, if you insist,
For now, God save the mark, he's growing old;
He's five and forty, and to hear him talk
These days you'd call him eighty; then you'd add
More years to that. He's old enough to be
The father of a world, and so he is.
"Ben, you're a scholar, what's the time of day?"
Says he and there shines out of him again
An aged light that has no name or station —
The mystery that's his — a mischievious
Half-mad serenity that laughs at fame
For being won so easy, and at friends
Who laugh at him for what he wants the most,
And for his dukedom down in Warwickshire. . . .

                    Lord! how I see him now,
Pretending, maybe trying, to be like us.
Whatever he may have meant, we never had him;
He failed us, or escaped, or what you will —
And there was that about him (God knows what —
We'd flayed another had he tried it on us)
That made as many of us as had wits
More fond of all his easy distances
Than one another's noise and clap your shoulder.

But think you not, my friend, he'd never talk!
Talk!   He was eldritch at it, and we listened,
Thereby acquiring much we knew before
About ourselves, and hitherto had held
Irrelevant, or not prime to the purpose. . . .

What has this to do with children? Well, when *is* a child? Who knows? I
could wish American poetry were as saturated with place-names and literary
names as is English poetry, that we had our "Banbury Cross" and "St Ives"
and "London Bridge," but we can wait. (We already have some good ex-
amples.) We can wait to become historical. What age child is this, do you
think?

"As I went up to London,"
I heard a stranger say —
Going up to London
In such a casual way.
He turned the magic phrase
That has haunted all my days
As if it were a common thing
For careless lips to say.
As he went up to London —
I'll wager many a crown
He never saw the road that I
Shall take to London Town.

When I go up to London,
'Twill be in April weather.
I'll have a riband in my rein
And flaunt a scarlet feather.
The broom will toss its brush for me,
Two blackbirds and a thrush will be
Assembled in a bush for me,
And sing a song together;
And all the blossomy hedgerows
Will shake their hawthorn down,
As I go riding, riding,
Up to London Town. . . .

Riding, riding eagerly,
Thrusting through the throng,
Traveling light, your Majesty,
Because the way was long.
I'll hurry fast to London gate —
The way was long and I am late —
I'll come at last to London gate,
Singing me a song.
Some old rhyme of ancient time
When wondrous things befell —

And there the boys and girls at play,
Understanding well,
Quick will hail me, clear and sweet,
Crowding, crowding after,
Every little crooked street
Will echo to their laughter,
Lilting as they mark my look,
Chanting two and two —
Dreamed it, dreamed it in a dream
And waked and found it true!

Sing, you rhymes, and ring, you chimes,
And swing, you bells of Bow!
When I go up to London,
All the world will know!

Certainly our children are at home in England, with Mother Goose and Lear and Blake and Stevenson's Lamplighter and De La Mare and Leslie Brooke and Humbert Wolfe and Milne — Milne! That indefatigable Christopher Robin! A fine companion but a tireless investigator! And he never walks — he always skips or twirls or stretches or "goes hippety-hoppety" or marches or dances or prances or steps so very carefully that he wears us out —

Whenever I walk in a London street,
I'm ever so careful to watch my feet;
       And I keep in the square,
       And the masses of bears,
Who wait in the corners all ready to eat
The sillies who tread on the lines of the street,
       Go back to their lairs,
       And I say to them, "Bears,
Just look how I'm walking in all of the squares!"

(When I was growing up, it was, "Step on a crack / Break your mother's back!" I consider this an improvement.) ·Sometime look through those Shepard illustrations in your Milne books and see if you can find one picture of an inactive child (or a grown-up or an animal, or a toy, for that matter) except the one for "Halfway down the stairs," — and I don't trust the expression on his face even there. I think this is a purely momentary halt. I remember very well the stir and excitement that first book caused when it came out, and one of my favorite recollections in the library is that of a girl's club in one of the children's rooms, dancing to these poems, as the librarian read the lines offstage. Such variety and naturalness! Have we become jaded, I wonder? Have we forgotten how good they are, how true to childhood?

Binker — what I call him — is a secret of my own,
And Binker is the reason why I never feel alone —

Children have their secret lives, and so do we, and each must be respected. Even as we read together and share our enjoyments, there can never be complete sharing. This is as true for two adults as for an adult and a child. So far-ranging a voyager is the free mind, so sensitive the memory to the merest touch, that we partake on at least two levels simultaneously. Not that the mind or the attention is divided — it is multiplied! Nor is it overlaid; it is not weighed down, but there is a very substantial underpinning placed beneath it by the memory or experience or the subconscious — whatever you choose to call it. It is the way you are listening now. You may not miss even a word, but there can be a sudden leap in the mind, an instantaneous journey of the memory even between two words. And how it enriches those words! Even while we are saying,

> "How many miles to Babylon?"
> "Threescore miles and ten."
> "Can I get there by candlelight?"
> "Yes, and back again,"

underneath it, flowing with the same rhythm, may run,

> "Does the road wind uphill all the way?"
> "Yes, to the very end."
> "Will the day's journey take the whole long day?"
> "From morn to night, my friend."

Even the question and answer form corresponds. Or it may be

> "I will make you brooches and toys for your delight
> Of bird-song at morning and star-shine at night.
> I will make a palace fit for you and me
> Of green days in forests and blue days at sea,"

and beneath it, for *you*, may be running

> "They told me, Heraclitus, they told me you were dead.
> They brought me bitter news to hear and bitter tears to shed.
> I wept as I remembered how often you and I
> Had tired the sun with talking and sent him down the sky"

— but the mood of delight is not broken; it is rather intensified by the living memory of a cherished friendship.

To me one of the greatest delights of poetry is this freedom to range through whatever body of it is familar to us, without regard for author or source or period of time. Such reflections not only sustain us, but occasionally

startle us with a sudden insight in places we had long considered well-known
territory. We seem to share in the act of creation. For a moment, we too
are makers, and this is to be encouraged, for it adds greatly to appreciation
and enjoyment. Of course it adds also to discouragement and fits of depression. We all suffer from it. Keats was not free from it — who is? "Why write,"
says he, "when Shakespeare has said it all? Even snails — look what he
says about snails!" And then we turn to Shakespeare and find even his im-
perturbability shaken, "desiring this man's art and that man's scope." Keats's
pathetic suggestion for his own epitaph, "Here lies one whose name is writ
in water," was beautifully interpreted and answered not long ago by one of
our modern poets —

> Only in water could your name be writ,
> Soft, bright, analogous, the element
> Of a consistency to compass it
> And speak continuously its rich intent.
> You thought the letters tracing went untold
> But the distinctive signature, aglow
> With purple, crimson, mignonette, and gold,
> Lies now upon the midnight's darkling flow
> And will translate, at dawn's awakening wave,
> To iridescent glassware of the sea.
> Who, being poet, mortally could crave
> A more enduring immortality
> Than that the waters of the earth proclaim,
> In movement and delight, his wistful fame?

I have kept, for the last, three pocket-pieces I want to make sure you take
with you. In speaking about the writing of poetry, "the figure a poem makes,"
Frost has said: "It begins in delight. It begins in delight and ends in wisdom."
That is our wish for childhood, too, for the life of every individual.

And this you will undoubtedly recognize:

> He who binds to himself a joy,
> Doth the winged life destroy.
> But he who kisses a joy as it flies
> Lives in eternity's sunrise.

And finally, as children and poetry respond to new influences, here is wisdom:

> Initiate the heart to change,
> For it is wiser so.
> Accepting the splendor of the hour,
> White with clematis or snow.
> Fortify the will with peace,
> No season taking root,
> Tranquil in mists, in warmth, in frost,
> Each bears fruit.

Book Selection for Children, Its Perplexities and Pleasures

By Elizabeth Nesbitt

IN ESSENCE, this talk is an expression of a belief that book selection for children should involve genuinely creative and valid literary criticism; an acknowledgment of the perplexities that attend the production of such criticism; an assertion that such literary criticism constitutes our highest professional achievement and our greatest professional pleasure.

Book selection is a double function. Books are selected first for the collection. Here a knowledge of the past in children's literature has more importance than is generally acknowledged, because only a knowledge of the past can give the perspective which produces penetrating literary criticism. A study of the development of children's literature reveals two things of the utmost relevancy to present day book selection. From Anglo-Saxon times to the present, writing for children has been strongly affected and at times determined by the dominant character and preoccupations of the period. The tender humaneness, the love of learning and liberality of idea, the enlightened theories of education so characteristic of the great humanists of the Renaissance are manifest in their writing. In complete contrast is the succeeding Puritan period, one of internal strife and struggle, of violent political and religious conflict, reflected in books which are, to us, horrifying in their morbidity. The turbulence of this period gave way before the easier, more leisured life of the succeeding era; the great middle class grew in number and power; social consciousness developed, and new theories of education came into being with emphasis on the virtues of industry, of reason, and of the useful. This period of highly developed moral and social consciousness, of glorification of reason, of conviction that only the utilitarian is worthwhile, inevitably produced the school of didactic writers, whose books demonstrated and illustrated their beliefs, and who, like the Puritans, but for a different reason, rejected the literature of the imagination. This period too faltered before the approach of new ideas. The emphasis on the purely utilitarian was succeeded by the belief that literature may and can exist for the sole purpose of giving pleasure and delight. The great creative literary critics began their interpretative writing, dealing with the intangibles which constitute true literature. Freedom of thought, idea, and form broke through all barriers and limitations, and the Golden Age of the late eighteenth and early nineteenth centuries arrived. It is this period which brings out forcibly the second and most important revelation afforded by a study of the past. It is only in an atmosphere of freedom from pressures, from the petty tyranny of small didacticisms, from the dictatorship of adult preoccupations, that genuine and lasting literature for children can be conceived and written.

The present is a period of tension, of confusion, even of fear. There have been such periods before. Out of such a time there will come some books which are, at the best ephemeral, at the worst distorted. There will come others which penetrate to fundamentals which underlie temporary confusions and which recreate some significant aspect of life beautifully and hopefully. Perspective gained from a sympathetic understanding of the past together with a clear perception of elements in the present which affect writing for children should simplify the perplexity of discriminating between the temporary, the insignificant, the merely didactic and the permanent, the significant, and the profoundly moral.

Presumably we have an advantage over the past in our greater knowledge of children, in our recognition that childhood is a way of life to which children are entitled, in our more extensive experience with children and books. Yet there remains the perplexity attendant upon our uncertain knowledge of what children want in books, upon our frequent inability to understand the extent of apprehension, not comprehension, with which a child reads a book. These perplexities need not be as confusing and insurmountable as they seem to be. We would have more certain knowledge of what children want in books if we had more penetrating insight into the reasons for the immortality of books like *Peter Rabbit, Treasure Island, Tom Sawyer, Little Women, Mary Poppins, The Little House in the Big Woods, The Borrowers.* Mere story does not account for the permanent hold these books have on the hearts and minds of children. I suggest for your thought that the love of generation after generation of children for some books is due to the way the books are written and to the fact that in some way they all "raise the curtain on the human heart," in Clifton Fadiman's phrase. Why does *Treasure Island* triumph over the universal dislike of the use of the first person? Why are *Mary Poppins* and *The Borrowers* so convincing that.child, and adult, live in the world of the book? *Little Women* has qualities which are considered today as grievous faults, and yet it has reached the status of a standard, if not a classic. Why? Yet how little written or spoken discussion of books goes beyond the inadequate "well written." or "beautifully written"; how little critical comment penetrates to the revelation of the human heart, the significant thing conveyed by plot and content. For a clear description of the vital difference, in reading, between apprehension and comprehension, I refer you to Sir Arthur Quiller-Couch's lecture on "Apprehension Versus Comprehension," one of the two lectures on children's literature contained in his *Art of Reading*. When we ask of children comprehension of anything that approaches greatness, we are requiring of them something which we ourselves cannot perform. As Sir Arthur Quiller-Couch says, true greatness is apprehensible little by little, never comprehensible immediately and at one time.

This is the thought which should be kept in mind in the second aspect of the double function of book selection — selection of a book for the child. The first aspect is possibly theoretical and remote. The second is immediate and actual, the final test of the collection and of the children's librarians' knowledge of books and of children. It calls for respect for children, for their insight, their ability to apprehend; for an appreciation of individual differences among children; for the realization that a rare book read with perception by a few children has value beyond that of an average book read by many children — and forgotten. It calls for an understanding of the chief function of the children's librarian as a book selector for children. To put into the children's hands the books they ask for is not her sole function. It is not enough to give the book wanted. The children's librarian must persuade children of perceptiveness and sensitivity to want the best we have. To paraphrase — it is not that our best books have been tried and found wanting. It is that they have been found difficult and not tried.

It is unlikely that books of quality can be introduced effectively if quality is submerged, for librarians and children, in a mass of books of easy but empty appeal, of ephemeral interest, of merely average quality. It is of the utmost importance that book selection should be considered a continuous process, one of constant re-evaluation. Only so can the perplexities and mistakes of initial book selection be mitigated and corrected. There is no realism in assuming that book selection, performed as new titles appear, can have unfailing validity. Large production, limitations of time imposed by book selection processes, lack of perspective, inability to try books with children, all these contribute to the trial and error aspect of selection of new titles. The advantages of periodic retrospective evaluation are apparent. The chief advantages are insight gained by use of books with children, perspective which a backward look always brings, the opportunity to exercise comparative judgment, the ability to apply fundamental critical principles which can be forgotten or misapplied too easily in the rush of initial selection, the privilege of more leisured re-reading, and the resultant renewal of conviction in the power of greatness to touch the human mind and spirit.

Discerning selection for the collection, for the child, and sound, rightly critical re-evaluation of books are all based on the understanding of what books can and should do for children, on the understanding and intelligent application of fundamental critical considerations as they pertain to various kinds of books, on appreciation of the meaning of the phrase "building a collection."

Library work for children was founded on the belief that the most underprivileged child — and privilege is not synonymous with material comforts and possessions — may win, through books read in childhood, something that will last all his life long; something not easily describable but compounded of many things — something kind and quiet which will sustain him all his days, because it is in part a warm inner security, a secret memory of lovely, enchanted things, a haunting recollection of beauty, an ineradicable perception of fundamental right and wrong. But even the most intelligent and responsive child cannot gain this rightful heritage of childhood if the inane, the trivial, and the insignificant is too easily accessible to him. Several years ago at the Richmond Conference there was given a talk impressively called "The Menace of Mediocrity." Some of the things said are unforgettable.

> The so-called average person is not average all the time.
> Mediocrity is a state of being, acquired almost imperceptibly by the easy, gradual acceptance of obvious standards.
> The point I would make is that in considering the average man, in establishing his identity by surveys, meeting his tastes in not too difficult books, keeping a collection within his range, even establishing rooms where he will encounter only average books, we have shown an unpleasant encouragement of mediocrity.

The fostering and cultivation of intelligence would seem to be fully as important as the attempt to make the best of non-intelligence. We would do well to insist that our book collections must be such as to satisfy the potentialities of the most intelligent of the children who use our libraries, and to re-assert that the appreciation of the finest children's literature by even a few children is worth more than the non-creative reading of the mediocre by many.

Understanding of true criticism recognizes that there are general critical principles which are relevant to any book. But it also recognizes that certain other considerations cannot be generalized — details, incidents, points of view, attitudes, characterizations. All these must be placed in context with the total spirit, intention, and final impression of a book as an entity. These qualities are variables, and should be judged, not in and for themselves, but in relation to the spirit, the meaning, the entirety of the book. A book must be judged by its totality, not by its parts. Critical judgment should originate in the total impression left after the perceptive reading of a book, and secondarily should be concerned with the way that total impression has been achieved.

Again, creative criticism recognizes that each kind of book has its individual requirements. Re-evaluation should be undertaken with an awareness of the uniqueness pertaining to each type of literature. In realistic fiction, some aspect of life should be presented wholly and honestly, with convincing sincerity, with authentic, inescapable realism. This accomplishment is the real reason for the wide appeal of Laura Ingalls Wilder's books. Realism which purports to be such and yet distorts actuality is inartistic and harmful. Historic fiction, at its best, is a meaningful recreation of a period, an incident, a person, based upon the author's complete control of his material, but going beyond mere accuracy of background to the perception and interpretation of the significance of the historic background. This double accomplishment constitutes the greatness of *Johnny Tremaine*. Fantasy must be the creation of power of imagination, not of mere fancy. The world within the book, no matter how other worldly or how fantastic it may be, must be convincing, because it is credible within its incredibility, plausible within its implausibility, rational within its irrationality. A second inherent requirement of fantasy is originality. This is necessarily so, because to be convincing, fantasy must be emotionally persuasive; to be persuasive it must be sincere; to be sincere, it must be the expression of an individual mind and temperament. Creativity of imagination, and originality must of necessity be accompanied by power of expression. The great writers of fantasy give life and form to abstractions, to ideas, to the intangibles, to the seemingly unattainable. The requirements of fantasy are such that there is no room for mediocrity. A fantasy, by its very nature is great or totally unacceptable. An adventure story should conform to the requirements of its type. A refined pirate story is an anomaly, rightly rejected by such children as the boy who said "When I read a pirate story, I want the decks to run with gore." Adventure on the whole is amoral, since the very nature of many kinds of adventure precludes preoccupation with morals and convention. Yet how often in our judgment of such books, we become mired in the bog of confused consideration of ethical principles. There is an essay by Robert Louis Stevenson called "A Gossip on Romance," which should be read by every children's librarian. Like many critical essays, it is immensely illuminating. Stevenson is talking about the kind of story we call adventure. One of his most striking comments is this:

> Drama is the poetry of conduct; romance the poetry of circumstance. — There is a vast deal in life and letters both which is not immoral, but simply a-moral; which either does not regard the human will at all, or deals with it in obvious and healthy relations; where the interest turns, not upon what a man shall choose to do but on how he manages to do it; not on the passionate slips and hesitations of the conscience, but on the problems of the body and of the practical intelligence, in clear, open-air adventure, the shock of arms or the diplomacy of life.

I sometimes wonder if *Treasure Island* would get into collections today, were it not haloed with traditional acceptance as a classic and with reverence for Stevenson's name. After all, the villain, Long John Silver, is the real hero of that book. A literary biography should present to the child a person who is worth writing about, and who is distinguished for what he was or for what he did; a person through whose life the child can enter a little further into the mystery and drama of personality. By use of authentic biographical technique, such a figure must be well rounded, real, vital, stepping out of the pages of the book a human, living being.

There are two types of non-fiction which will reveal themselves in the re-evaluation of books. One is the important and necessary book which gives needed information. Some of these books are obviously ephemeral since recency of correct information is essential to their value. But there are other books of non-fiction which deal with non-dated material and which underline information with vitality, with wonder and curiosity and enthusiasm.

The phrase "building a collection" was once in frequent use. It is less often seen and heard today, when the emphasis seems rather to be upon selection of individual books and groups of books. It may well be that library schools have contributed to the focussing of attention on selection of individual books as an end in itself rather than upon the additional contribution the single book makes to the structure which is the book collection. Both the content and method of book courses may foster a disintegrated view of a multitude of fragments rather than a vision of an inter-related and inter-dependent whole. It is essential in such courses to achieve order by considering books individually and in relation to their kind. But after the breakdown, the patterns governing the collection as a whole may not be apparent.

The core of every children's book collection, the nucleus about which the rest of the collection is built, is the group of books which have passed the test of time, the books which have proved themselves classics.

Surrounding the nucleus of classics is a circle of books which might be called standards. These are books which with the passage of time may become classics, or books which may never become true classics but which have such positive qualities as to cause their defects to be of minor importance. Like the classics, many of them are duplicated in great numbers. Like the classics, there is something within the group for every child, though not every book is for every child.

It has been said that some classics, and also some standards, have the power of immediate and wide appeal, and that others will need slow and skillful introduction. It is also true that the child must be accepted as he is at the moment. The child who has known the picture books of Caldecott and Brooke, *Timothy Turtle*, the small classics of Beatrix Potter, the stories of A. A. Milne, and *Deep Wood* is ready for *Wind in the Willows*. But the child who has not been so happy in his introduction to reading, will not be ready for Grahame's book, unless he is one of those endowed with instinctive appreciation of the rare. Consequently a third and important circle of books is essential. These are what used to be called the stepping-stone books. It is they which constitute, at any time in the continuing book selection process, the most difficult and dangerous perplexity. It is not hard to recognize either the superior book or the inexcusably inferior book. It is by no means inevitably easy to recognize when the strong outweighs the weak; to realize that this particular book offers something constructive in the way of meeting an interest, satisfying a need, or acting as a stimulant to broaden interests, enhance appreciation, or to introduce better books. This is the main design of the book collection for children, three groups of books, the third being so selected as to guide children to the second and first.

It is curious how the wisdom of the past continues to illuminate the problems of the present. The ultimate purpose toward which our judgment of new books, reevaluation of older books, and construction of a total collection should be directed is given more than adequate expression in the words of Matthew Arnold:

> The great need in modern culture, which is scientific in method, rationalistic in spirit, and utilitarian in purpose, is to find some effective agency for cherishing within us the ideal. That is, I take it, the business and function of literature. Literature alone will not make a good man. Nor would I pretend for a moment that literature can be any substitute for life and action. It is life that is the great educator. But books — if they are well chosen — awake within us the diviner mind, and rouse us to a consciousness of what is best in ourselves and others.

If our books are well chosen, so as to cherish within children the ideal, and to arouse within them a consciousness of what is best in others and in themselves, we shall gain a compensating professional pleasure and satisfaction in spite of the perplexities attendant upon the selection. It is the exercise of literary criticism and the articulate expression of the results of that criticism that constitute one of the creative aspects of our profession. We admire and envy those who through the possession of high talents and of the creative imagination can write a great book, compose great music, paint a great picture. We forget that it is also an art and an act of the creative imagination to read perceptively, to listen appreciatively, and to see with a truly observing eye. It is our professional privilege and should be our professional pleasure to view as an art the wise choosing of individual books and the building of a book collection which, because of the excellence of the structure as a whole, will bring to fruition the central philosophy of library work with children — faith in the efficacy of literature to instill fundamental truths by example rather than by precept, by persuasion rather than by dictation, by interpretation of truth rather than by mere, unimaginative presentation of facts.

A book collection designed to fulfill this philosophy will bring another pleasure, more personal, and less easy to define in concrete terms. Library work with children is not a profession in which to look for immediate and measurable results. The revelation which a particular child may find in a particular book is a private and personal thing, and not a thing to be intruded upon. And yet, because of the special kind of love a child has for a book which is uniquely his, we are occasionally granted certainty of the highest achievement we can attain — and none the less high because it is impossible to translate it into statistics or even into the form of a statement in annual reports. No cost is to great to pay for the knowledge that we have given even a few children uninhibited joy through nonsense — that we have given one child the exhilaration and release brought by a life-long love of poetry — that, through biography we have suggested, another child has sensed the complexity and paradoxically the simplicity of a human being, has glimpsed the heights of being and doing of which a human being is capable — that through such books as *Johnny Tremaine* and *Big Tiger and Christian* a few children have perceived the mystery of human destiny — that we have led one child from *Peter Rabbit* to *Deep Wood* to *Wind in the Willows* to *The Hobbit* to Tolkien's great and magnificent trilogy — that we have led another through the nursery classics, folk and fairy tales, myths and legends to the cosmic implications of the great world epics.

Mediocrity is a state of being, acquired almost imperceptibly by the easy, gradual acceptance of obvious standards.

We owe to ourselves as well as to the children we serve refusal to acquire such a state, refusal to take the easy way of gradual acceptance of mediocre and obvious standards. And if the other way is difficult, beset with perplexities, it provides the zestful pleasure of challenge and stimulation, the invigorating pleasure of putting to good use knowledge, intelligence and discriminatory power.